EXPOSED
HYPOCRISY IN HIGH PLACES

BLITZ EDITIONS

Published by Blitz Editions
an imprint of Bookmart Ltd
Registered Number 2372865
Trading as Bookmart Ltd
Desford Road
Enderby
Leicester LE9 5AD

ISBN 1 85605 212 5

This material has previously appeared in *Inside Stories*.

Every effort has been made to contact the copyright holders for the pictures.
In some cases they have been untraceable, for which we offer our apologies.
Special thanks to the Hulton-Deutsch Collection, who supplied the majority of pictures,
and thanks also to the following libraries and picture agencies:
Rex Features, Syndication International, Topham Picture Source

This book was produced by Amazon Publishing Limited
Designed by Cooper Wilson Design
Edited by Graham McColl

Printed in the Slovak Republic
51724

EXPOSED
HYPOCRISY IN HIGH PLACES

MAYFLOWER MADAM
Sydney Biddle Barrows

Sydney Biddle Barrows' girls provided very discreet personal services to some of the highest earners in New York. And when she was finally taken to court, it was the authorities, and not Sydney, who were to end up being embarrassed in public.

New York is a city that caters to all tastes and styles; every whim, every fancy, every facet of life, both high and low. In the glittering penthouses of Park Avenue, the bistros of Greenwich Village, the ornate town houses of the Upper West Side, absolutely everything is available – at a price.

No wonder that in the cash rich 1980s, when money flowed out of Wall Street and the other financial centres of the world, prostitution went upmarket to cash in on the new-rich. In the underbelly of the Big Apple existed the street hookers, the five-and-dime tarts who would turn tricks in cars in remote parking lots or in cheap flophouse motels. But these weren't the girls that were attractive to travelling businessmen with expense accounts from the office and a loving family at home.

High-class hookers were the new money-spinning business – girls who looked like models and behaved like ladies... except in the bedroom. And no-one cashed in on the money-for-high-class-sex racket more than a woman who became known as The Mayflower Madam. Her little black book contained more secrets than a Pentagon computer, more potential damage than an arsenal of H-bombs. To this day, the Mayflower Madam has not revealed the scandals that lay within her impressive client list. The cops put her out of business. And, so far, she is the only one involved in this affair who has suffered.

The Mayflower Madam – alias Sydney Biddle Barrows – catered to the highest of high society. There were several chief executive officers of Wall Street companies. There were Arab princes, judges, a British rocker, a Hollywood film producer, a professional opera singer, a Catholic priest who smoked marijuana, an Orthodox Rabbi, bankers, brokers, deal makers, shakers and movers in the swirling Big Apple of the 1980s. And they were catered to by girls called Paige, whose father was a diplomat, and Margot, whose daddy was a judge. Sydney's skill was in matching high class merchandise to high-class payers – and it was a magic formula that worked every time. These stunning girls, dressed in

Above: *Looking more like a society hostess than a supplier of good-time girls, Sydney Biddle Barrows heads for an appointment with justice.*

Opposite: *A glass of champagne for the Mayflower Madam, the blueblood who went into history as the most famous brothel keeper in America.*

designer silk and *always* wearing stockings beneath (her strict orders) accompanied their 'Johns' to dinners hosted by men like Henry Kissinger, to United Nations balls, to ambassadorial functions and to glittering charity dinners costing £10,000 a head. In Sydney's words: 'I only ever picked the really attractive ones – and in return they got classy, attractive, successful guys. Most single women in Manhattan would have killed to go out with them.'

Sydney Biddle Barrows, the blue-blood so named because her first ancestors sailed on the Mayflower to America hundreds of years before, thought she had hit on the perfect business. 'Everyone was happy,' she said. 'The dates were so pleasant for the girls that often they were late back – having given the client some extra time for free because they were enjoying themselves so much. Often they came back and said: "I can't believe I'm getting paid for this!"'

When she was eventually busted, the question on everybody's lips was: How did this demure, single-strand pearl necklace-wearing schoolmarm get into the sleazy world of prostitution? But Sydney insists there was really nothing difficult – in a moral or business sense – to it at all. 'The American public has been fed a lot of lies. People think the girls were degraded – that simply wasn't true. The girls who worked for me never were, I made sure of it. I kind of drifted into this business, but once I was in it, found out that I enjoyed it very much. And I was good at it.'

THE OLDEST PROFESSION

Boarding schools, debutante balls, society dinners – this was the lot of Sydney Biddle Barrows before she went into the oldest profession in the world. She had completed a course in merchandising and business management at Manhattan's Fashion Institute of Technology and was working in the city in the early 1980s as a buyer for a company that shipped merchandise to clothes and fashion-accessory boutiques all over the world. 'It was quite a good job,' she said, 'but leaving it – well, I had my mind made up for me by the boss. He asked me to off-load some unfashionable handbags because he was on the take. It was a real dilemma. I knew if I didn't distribute the handbags I would be out of a job. But at the same time I was horrified and scared about getting into trouble with the police. So I quit and found myself out of a job. Then next thing I know is I am answering phones for an escort agency for $50 a night, something that was arranged through a friend. It really looked like fun, something lucrative and a real challenge.'

She became fascinated with the whole call-girl game. It struck her as odd that you could get phone sex, kinky sex in Greenwich Village, child pornography in the sleazy parlours that dotted Times Square – but nowhere was there a market for a man and a woman to get together to form a discreet liaison. She went on: 'When you think of all the dangers that street girls faced from weirdos, from disease, from danger, from being busted – when I eventually went into business there

Below: *The Mayflower, the ship that brought Biddle Barrows' ancestors to the New World from the old. Those puritans would surely have turned in their graves at the thought of her chosen profession.*

was more chance of my girls being killed in a cab crash than meeting up with a pervert. I realised that this isn't for everyone, that ethics are in the eye of the beholder. I don't smoke, for example – to me, that's a disgusting habit. I don't gamble. Those are my moral choices. Those are my personal moral choices.

'When we went into business I found out that most of the clients worked as hard as the girls. They had to give the girls a glamorous and fun and exciting experience or they couldn't be clients. Believe it or not, that's true. And it's not true that the girls didn't enjoy it. The majority enjoyed it the majority of the time. They're just ordinary girls, articulate, fun, warm, honest, nice people with goals in life who just needed a little extra money.

'When people ask me about how I got into this business I tell them the story of a girlfriend of mine who works for a big public relations firm. She got a big promotion and called me up excitedly: "Sydney, I'm so excited! I have been offered this fabulous account with Stolichnaya, the Russian vodka." I said: "You're not going to take it, are you? You're not seriously considering it?" She said: "Of course, why wouldn't I?" I said: "You're talking about a commu-

nist product, where the money goes back into a country that is trying to destroy us. How could you possibly do that?" She didn't see it that way at all, but I would never have taken that job in a billion years. I don't care if they had offered me four times as much money as I was making. You see – people have different values.'

BRANCHING OUT

With her conscience assuaged on such difficult moral issues, Sydney and her friend who had first got her into the dial-a-girl business decided to branch out on their own. But they decided it would be strictly classy, A-list people all the way. She placed ads in such magazines as the *Village Voice* – the avant garde newspaper that served the funky Greenwich Village area of the city and which was read by newcomers to town who were looking for work and apartments – and also in *Show Business*, a magazine for those in the entertainment trade, looking for 'high-toned girls'.

Once the girls had been selected the adverts for an 'escort agency' went into such quality newspapers as the *International Herald Tribune* and the *New York Times*. Then she did some market

'THE CLIENTS... HAD TO GIVE THE GIRLS A GLAMOROUS AND FUN AND EXCITING EXPERIENCE OR THEY COULDN'T BE CLIENTS'

Below: *The bright lights of the big city – Manhattan, with the towers of the Brooklyn Bridge in the foreground. Such wealth meant many clients seeking sex – at a price.*

research of her own – scrutinising the pitfalls, traps and operating procedures of the other bordellos in town. Calling herself Sheila Devin, she traipsed around escort agencies on the pretext of getting a job – but really honing her skills about the game, deciding what she would and wouldn't do when it came to running her own stable of luscious, willing young things. And she was in business – as simple as that.

The girls, whose maximum age was 25, were instructed on how to behave, how to dress, how to deport themselves, how to get past hotel security guards (dress like a young business executive carrying a briefcase – with the case containing the credit-card machine that they would need to take a client's money) and even what lingerie to wear. The girls were instructed to be courteous at all times, demure, coy and charming.

It was entirely up to them what sex acts they got up to – although there was a sliding-scale of fees depending on any particular client's 'preferences'. And she also told them how to check for certain types of sexually transmitted diseases, if they were at all dubious about going to bed with a customer. Sydney said they were housewives, college kids, models, students and aspiring actresses. And they were all spellbound by their new madam's sales-pitch that they were going to be the *crème de la crème* of night ladies about to take Manhattan by storm!

HIGH DIVIDENDS

The operation was run out of an apartment on the Upper West Side of town, the ritziest neighbourhood for what many still say is the lowest profession. Soon the calls were coming thick and fast. Because Sydney operated on a grapevine network – clients telling other potential clients – there was always an element of risk when the agency started, in 1981, that it might take some time to really get going. But in her case, the well-chosen women and 'discretion at all costs' began to pay high dividends.

Soon high rollers, particularly men from the Middle East, began shelling out thousands a night for girls. 'Those guys would order girls like they were pizzas,' she said.

'They'd have several in one sitting and still come back for more.' As well as receiving a percentage for each 'trick' booked by Sydney, there were lavish gifts heaped on them by the grateful men they satisfied – everything from costume jewellery and perfume to expensive watches and gems by Rolex and Cartier.

An interesting sideline to the nocturnal activities of the Mayflower Madam only emerged after her arrest on prostitution charges. For five years she had been seeing a psychoanalyst in an effort to make herself 'like myself better'.

She explained: 'It was nothing to do with the business I was in. My father left us when I was four. He is some guy that everyone says is my father but I just never knew the man. I'm sure that had a lot to do with my being unhappy and having negative images about myself. It's one thing for parents to be divorced, but my father's attitude was that if he wasn't married to my mother anymore then the kids didn't exist either.

'I mean, how do you explain to someone who is four years old that your own father doesn't call for your birthday or Christmas? We were from the only broken home I knew about. I told my therapist all about it but he wasn't bothered about it at all. In fact I was rather proud of what I was

Above: *Dancing in Stringfellows nightclub with William Novak, her biographer.*

Right: *Tom Bird, another eligible bachelor, dances with the celebrated madam after her arrest.*

SHE DENIED THAT SHE WAS SOMEHOW TAKING REVENGE ON MEN BY GETTING GIRLS TO CHARGE THEM FOR SEX

---

doing. I got a lot out of it professionally and personally.' She denied allegations, levelled later, that she was somehow taking revenge against men by getting girls to charge them for sex – a scheme concocted because of her father's departure.

She scoffed at any psycho-babble explanations of her work. 'I simply enjoyed it and was good at booking the best for the girls,' she said. Was she never tempted to go on to the shop floor, as it were, herself? 'Absolutely not,' she said. 'After all, Lee Iaccoca ran Chrysler and he never made a car on the production line!'

The money continued rolling in at an impressive rate of knots for the Mayflower Madam – her girls charged $1,000 (approximately £750) – for sex with clients, and more for 'extras,' which might include kinky sex, or overtime. Quite how much she earned has always been shrouded in mystery, but it's believed that she kept over £100,000 of her immoral earnings, profits after she was arrested.

Sydney was 32 in 1984, and her prostitution business was two years old, when she was finally arrested. Out of the hundreds of

they could not go after me. They made this big publicity splash about me and all the Mayflower connections.'

She was arrested and led away in chains in a night-time bust. The press had been tipped off and they had a field day – never had they seen the proprietor of a whore-house so demurely dressed in a grey flannel business suit with a petite figure and a ready smile. Instantly she was recognised as something different from the usual madam busted by the city's vice squads. But it was not so much her personal appearance or the number of girls she con-trolled that interested the press – it was *who* the girls had been with that set tabloid newspapers in the Big Apple clamouring for the secrets of the little black book with all the names. A source in District Attorney Robert Morgenthau's office said: 'It's dynamite. She's got the A-team of com-merce, foreign royalty and showbiz in there.' Bids for the names soared into six figures, then over $1,000,000. But Sydney's own code of morals protected – and continues to protect – those 'gentle-men' who sought out her girls. She says: 'I could never, ever reveal who they were. They were men buying a service, that's all, a service that happened to be sex. I couldn't ever betray that trust.

Above and Right: *Sydney was never a shrinking violet – preferring to defend her trade in flesh, and always insisting that her girls enjoyed the line of work they were in.murder.*

streetwalkers, the dozens of bordellos, the innumerable back street cat-houses, hers was the one that was chosen – because of the neighbourhood it was in and due to her irate landlord.

He became concerned at the number of girls coming and going from the premises each night – the girls bringing back their credit card receipts to the 'madam' and picking up fresh instructions of where to go, or merely to be inspected to make sure they matched up to Miss Barrows' high standards of dress and deportment. She says angrily now: 'In order to get the police to move in this the landlord had to exagger-ate. He had to make me sound so big that

'I think the prosecutors expected me to throw myself upon their mercy or something but I wouldn't give them that satisfaction. They tried to get me to feel bad about the girls – saying that I had corrupted them. But I told them that just as there can be people who drink socially and not become drunks, so there can be call girls who are call girls with no ill effects. It's a personal, moral decision. I told them: "Why shouldn't sex be for sale if a girl wants to do it?" It's not the oldest profession for nothing and what do these so called experts know anyway? I held my head up high when I was arrested.'

Friends threw defence-fund money-spinning balls, eager to help out with her soaring legal bills which would mount by the day and eventually top out at something over $300,000. She was facing numerous felony counts which could have put her in prison for up to seven years.

A SPLENDID VICTORY

The case rapidly became an embarrassment to the city as massive media interest from around the world made the whole investigation something of a laughing stock. The police were castigated for booking a madam in a city where there are routinely between 15 and 20 murders a night – wouldn't their time be better spent in getting their priorities right, it was argued?

Eventually, nine months later, her case was plea-bargained down to a single count of promoting prostitution – what the defence would later term a 'kiss on the wrist' punishment – and she was fined just $5,000. The deal saved her from prison – and also saved the lucrative book and TV deals which she would have been banned from pursuing had she been behind bars. All in all, it was a splendid victory for her.

Life after scandal has been kind to the Mayflower Madam, but the tag which ensured her continuing success as a scarlet woman is now one she would like to put behind her. Not for any reasons of shame or disgrace – just that she wants to move into writing, or designing or, more recently, lecturing. But there are never any regrets.

She said: 'Would I do it all again? Sure, of course I would. What happened that was so bad? I got busted? So what? Am I dead? Blind? Don't I still have both my arms?

Have I lost any friends? Doesn't my family still love me? Don't I still have a wonderful future ahead of me? I can't find one negative thing to think about it, not one.

'They were heady times. It was like a sorority house. It wasn't some sordid, weird, grimy business. There was an esprit de corps that was just marvellous between me and the girls. One thing I always liked was taking them to wonderful stores in New York, like Saks Fifth Avenue, where I would buy them wonderful outfits. It really uplifted my heart to see them kitted out in glamorous clothes, the kind they only ever

Above: *Two V for victory signs from Sydney after she learns that there is no prison cell awaiting her.*

'WOULD I DO IT ALL AGAIN? SURE, OF COURSE I WOULD. WHAT HAPPENED THAT WAS SO BAD?'

Above: *The champagne was good, but nothing tasted sweeter to Sydney than freedom.*

Opposite Top: *Another party pose with Bird. Sydney achieved immortality in America and now lectures on such topics as bedroom manners and how women should dress for their men.*

Opposite Below: *A final victory pose for the woman who took sex out of the bedroom and onto prime-time news programmes.*

used to dream about. It was like summer camp and college all rolled into one. No, like Edith Piaf, I have no regrets.'

In the years immediately following the scandal Sydney wrote a book, and enjoyed a career as a £2,000 a night speaker, travelling around America giving lectures on business success and tips on etiquette – combined, of course, with the lurid tales of when she was America's most famous madam. 'I guess I will never entirely shake it off,' she said. 'If I died today my headstone, I am sure, would read: "Sydney Biddle Barrows – Mayflower Madam". But I hope that I might also be remembered for other things as well. I have achieved other things in my life, so everything is not all negative, not all just the "Mayflower Madam".'

She rolled her show out to places like Peoria, Illinois, Omaha and Kansas City – true

small town America where audiences blushed, giggled and winced at her tales of the high life. One of her most successful stories was telling the audiences what the successful hooker never left home without – make up, a spare pair of knickers, shower cap, pen and paper, cab fare home... and an aspirin in case of a headache while on the job!

TV FAME

In 1987, Candice Bergen, the famed Hollywood actress, played Sydney Biddle Barrows in a sanitised made-for-TV movie about her pimping success. Sydney also went on to write another book, this time an etiquette guide, most of it based in or around the bedroom. But even though she still has her Upper West Side apartment and all America knows – and remains intrigued by – her personality, a long term companionship still seems to evade her. Men don't want to date her, she said. 'I would never have thought the supply would dry up. But it's not worth it for men to get involved with someone so high profiled, I guess.'

Society too – the connections which allowed her to trade on the blueblood Mayflower connection – wants little to do with her. The Mayflower Society, a snooty sect of social climbers in New York, has barred its door to her and she finds that the invitations to show up at the kind of high-class affairs that her high-class girls went to have also evaporated. The Social Register, a kind of who's who of American elite, dropped her and her mother after the scandal broke. And her grandfather, Donald Byers Barrows, said of her shortly after the arrest: 'I have a great many grandchildren, and had them all over to visit several years ago. But Sydney's attitude was very poor then. Always has been. I am not really interested in seeing her after what she has done. I just dismiss her ongoing notoriety as an unpleasant thing in my mind.'

Love her or loathe her, approve of her or damn her, she remains right about one thing – 'Here lies the Mayflower Madam' could well end up as the epitaph on Sydney Biddle Barrows' tombstone.

JEFFREY ARCHER
An Identity Crisis

When a British newspaper printed a story about an alleged encounter between the Conservative Party chairman Jeffrey Archer and a prostitute, he fought back fiercely. The country held its breath as the sordid allegations were dragged through court.

I t was quite the most extraordinary scandal to rock the British establishment in many a year.

Jeffrey Archer, boyishly handsome deputy chairman of the Tory party and beloved standard-bearer of the faith in the shires and the counties – who rallied the troops on behalf of his faithful prime minister Margaret Thatcher – had, quite simply, been caught at the centre of a scandal involving a prostitute. Although totally innocent of ever having met the woman in question – let alone having slept with her – Archer did the decent thing by immediately resigning his position.

But his decision to step down in October 1986, and his statement that he had never met vice-girl Monica Coghlan, did not spell the end of the matter. Instead, libelled by a national newspaper that he had indeed known her, his fight to clear his name went to the highest court in the land – and with it unravelled one of the most intriguing stories ever heard in a British court.

At its end Jeffrey Archer, now Lord Archer, was totally vindicated and the *Daily Star* newspaper was poorer to the tune of £500,000 plus costs – the biggest libel damages award in British history. And it had all happened because Jeffrey Archer, in being a thoroughly decent chap, had tried to help a woman pleading on the phone to him, and had become embroiled in a plot that involved a vice girl, a dubious witness to an encounter that never happened, and a Sunday newspaper.

The world awoke to the scandal on Sunday 26 October 1986. On the front page of the scandal sheet *The News of the World*, and on further pages inside, there unravelled an extraordinary story of how an associate of Mr. Archer – a man named Robert Stacpoole – had gone to platform three at Victoria railway station in the heart of London to hand over money to a waiting prostitute.

The prostitute, Monica Coghlan, was taking the money to 'go away' on holiday for a while. Long range cameras supplied the photos of the cash being handed over while inside the pages of the newspaper were curious tape recordings, allegedly made between Monica – calling herself 'Debbie', the name she used when 'working' – and Mr. Archer. The conversations, which will be examined later in the context of the amazing court case which was to follow, apparently had Mr. Archer offering to set up money through an intermediary to pay for her to go on holiday. *The News of the World* did NOT say he had slept with a prostitute, or that he had known her. It did, however, print sections of conversations between Coghlan and him in which she said she was being 'pressured' by a third party to 'spill the beans' on an alleged night of love between her and Archer – something that he vehemently denied.

UNANSWERED QUESTIONS

The world was left with the curious, unanswered question as to why a man at the pinnacle of public life in Britain would arrange for a prostitute to go away on holiday if he had never met her. For Archer, who resigned his job on the day of the scandal, the answer was an easy one. It was clear that someone was trying to implicate him with this woman and that she was in trouble. In order to get her away from the third party he would pay her expenses for a holiday.

His statement said: 'I have never, repeat never, met Monica Coghlan, nor have I ever had any association of any kind with a prostitute.' Yes, he might have been guilty of foolishness. Yes, his marriage would survive. But his career was in tatters and there seemed little left for him to do but to go back to writing his extremely successful novels and plays and retire from public life.

Opposite: *Jeffrey Archer, a favourite of Mrs Thatcher's, was caught up in the maelstrom of a wicked plot that ended in his resignation.*

Below: *Mrs Thatcher, who valued Archer beyond words.*

HIS FIGHT TO CLEAR HIS NAME UNRAVELLED ONE OF THE MOST INTRIGUING STORIES EVER HEARD IN A BRITISH COURT

Above: *Mary and Jeffrey Archer sip champagne in the garden of their Cambridge home after their victory.*

Right: *Lloyd Turner , the silent editor of the* **Daily Star***, who refused to go into the witness box to give evidence during the trial.*

CALM AND COLLECTED, MARY SHOWED TRUE COURAGE AS SLUR AFTER UNSUBSTANTIATED SLUR WAS LEVELLED AT HER HUSBAND

But a week later the *Daily Star* newspaper, under the supervision of its editor Mr. Lloyd Turner, printed a page one story under the headline 'Poor Jeffrey!' It was the story of a friend of Monica, talking about how Monica had told her about the encounter with Jeffrey Archer. And that was the *Daily Star*'s fatal error which would land them in court and cost them such massive damages.

The News of the World had been meticulously careful NOT to draw any such link. It provided its readers with tape extracts, photos and a diary of events leading up to the pay-off at Victoria Station. Nowhere was there a mention that he had ever known her for the simple reason that they could never prove such a thing. The *Daily Star* could not prove it either – and it would cost them dear.

When the story broke, Jeffrey Archer discussed it with his brilliant and loyal wife Mary at their home near Cambridge and decided that resorting to law was the only course open to them. It would be painful, it would mean putting themselves up to scrutiny in the highest court in the land. But he was innocent – and he was determined to clear his name.

It was not until July the following year that Archer vs the *Daily Star* and Lloyd Turner was finally heard at the Law Courts in the Strand, the venerable high temple of justice in Britain. It was theatre of the highest order, the court case of the year that had queues lining up as dawn broke over London trying for a few public seats in the pathetically small court, to witness the spectacle. And it would prove to be a shining victory for Archer, a humiliation for Fleet Street and a rout for Monica Coghlan.

Arriving with Archer that first day was wife Mary – the hitherto private woman whose courage in coming forward to stand by her man earned her the respect of the nation. Calm and collected, she showed true courage as slur after unsubstantiated slur was levelled at him.

The only time she ever looked at all pensive or worried was on the first day of proceedings, Monday 6 July 1986, when the tape recordings were played to a hushed court. Afterwards, Archer denied having met Coghlan in Shepherd Market in September. He also denied going with her to a hotel called the Albion where they had sex and denied that he had ever met her. Archer hired the most brilliant libel litigator in Britain, Mr. Robert Alexander, Q.C., who said that Archer had paid her money for two reasons.

One was that he needed time to stop an 'evil man' spreading lies about him, and the second that he genuinely felt sorry for the prostitute who was beginning to become hounded by the press.

These are the sensational extracts from the tape recorded conversations between Coghlan and Archer that were played on

the first day of his libel trial against the *Star*. The first was recorded on 25 September 1986, and the reader should bear in mind that Mr. Archer has no idea that Monica Coghlan is in cahoots with *The News of the World* as she makes the calls.

TAPE A: Extracts from their telephone calls on 25 September 1985.
COGHLAN: I don't know if you remember me, this is Debbie here...
ARCHER: Who?
COGHLAN: Debbie...
ARCHER: No, I'm sorry, have you got the right number?
COGHLAN: Well I met you in Shepherd Market a few weeks ago and we went back to Victoria, there was a gentleman there when we was leaving. He's giving me a lot of hassle. He's telling me who you are and he's been offering me money. I don't want anything to do with this. I just want this guy off my back. I've got a two year old son you know, I live up North...
ARCHER: I'm sorry, you must have the wrong number. Who do you think you are speaking to?
COGHLAN: Archer, Mr. Archer...
ARCHER: Yes you are but...
COGHLAN: Well he told me who you were, right, and he put a proposition to me about money, but I don't, I don't want to know any of this, I just want this guy off my back.
ARCHER: Well, I'm awfully sorry but I don't know who you are and I don't know who he is, but of course if he was saying that I would tell the police straight away.
COGHLAN: You would tell the police...?
ARCHER: Of course I would, because it's not true and I don't even know who you are. I'm awfully sorry, but I've never met you and I don't know who you are.
COGHLAN: He said he recognised you, right?
ARCHER: What's his name?
COGHLAN: It's like a foreign name, Kurtha, or something like that. He said that he thinks you recognised him. He just won't leave me alone. I'm really frightened.
ARCHER: Well I'm awfully sorry, I don't know you. I don't know him. It's a ridiculous suggestion and I suggest you go to the police.
COGHLAN: To the police...?

ARCHER: I certainly would if anyone suggested it was me. I wouldn't hesitate to go to the police.
COGHLAN: All my family, they don't know what I do. They think I come to London on business. I just want this flaming guy off my back. He said he knows you very well.
ARCHER: Well, I'm awfully sorry, it wasn't me on that night, whenever night it was. 'Cos I don't know you at all.
COGHLAN: I met you in Shepherd Market. You approached me. You said you'd rather get your car and pick me up and in the meantime this other guy came up to me and I... I... told him how much it is and everything. I got into his car and then when I came out of the hotel with him, you was parked outside.
ARCHER: Well, I'm sorry, that's not me. It may well have been someone who looked like me. But it certainly wasn't me. And I'm very sorry you've made a bad mistake.
COGHLAN: He's shown me a picture of you and, you know, as far as I'm concerned it was you. Can't you just sort of make a call and get this guy off my bloody back?
ARCHER: Well, if you give me his name

Above: *Lord Justice Caulfield, the stern but fair judge who presided with equanimity and fairness over the libel trial.*

'IT MAY WELL HAVE BEEN SOMEONE WHO LOOKED LIKE ME. BUT IT CERTAINLY WASN'T ME'

and telephone number I will try.

COGHLAN: I haven't got his number with me, I left it at home. If I can give you his number could you just bloody get him off my back?

ARCHER: I certainly will, 'cos I shall put it in... I, I certainly will...

COGHLAN: Thank you very much. OK, I'll get back to you then.

TAPE B: Extracts from their telephone conversation on 2 October 1986.

COGHLAN: Is that Mr. Archer?

ARCHER: Speaking.

COGHLAN: Yes, this is Debbie here.

ARCHER: Oh yes.

COGHLAN: I spoke to you last week.

ARCHER: Yes you did.

COGHLAN: I've actually been staying with some friends in Manchester because I'm too scared to go to the house because there are reporters there.

ARCHER: If anyone says anything to you, stay very firm and say: 'I made a mistake. Now I have seen the picture more carefully, it wasn't him,' and that will be all right.

COGHLAN: But it was you, I've seen the picture, look...

ARCHER: I assure you, it was not me.

COGHLAN: Well, the picture they showed me was definitely...

ARCHER: Well, I'm sure it looked like me but it wasn't me. And you don't want to...

COGHLAN: Look, I don't want nothing from you or anybody else, right? I just want to be able to go home with my son, you know, and forget this whole bloody thing.

ARCHER: Well how, how can I help you?

COGHLAN: Well, can't you sort of meet me or something, or arrange something to get this guy off my...

ARCHER: You said you were going to tell me his name.

COGHLAN: But I can't get in the bungalow to get the number or his name.

ARCHER: I don't know what to do about it because it's really nothing to do with me and I am just trying to help you. Get his name and I will get him off your back.

COGHLAN: As far as I'm concerned I'm an innocent party, apart from my job.

ARCHER: I believe you totally and I also believe you wouldn't talk to anyone. And I admire you for that too.

COGHLAN: So you want me to ring you when I get...

ARCHER: If you can get the name of the person who's been bothering you...

COGHLAN: But he has got a picture... and it's outside, the car's parked outside the hotel. I've seen the picture with my own eyes.

ARCHER: Well, I assure you it's not me. But I would just say to you, if you speak, then they will print it.

COGHLAN: Yes.

ARCHER: Whatever you do they will print. Uhm, and if they catch you they will offer you a lot of money.

COGHLAN: Yeah.

ARCHER: You realise that?

COGHLAN: Well, I know, they've offered me money already. I don't want the money.

ARCHER: I think that's very good. I think you're a very honest and good person.

COGHLAN: Well, as soon as I can get the number I'll do what you said anyway.

ARCHER: And in return, I'm afraid that you'll have to say very firmly that you made a mistake. It certainly wasn't me and, uhm, don't tell them you've been in contact or there'll be more trouble.

TAPE C: Extracts from their telephone conversation on 23 October 1986.

COGHLAN: Hello, I spoke to you a couple of weeks ago.

ARCHER: Yes, you did.

COGHLAN: Apparently this Aziz Kurtha... uhm, he's made some kind of statement.

ARCHER: Yup.

COGHLAN: And he's going absolutely crazy to get hold of me.

ARCHER: Well, I think it's quietening down.

COGHLAN: It's quietening down?

ARCHER: I hear from the people who have been in touch with me that it is. But I think that you will have to stay out of sight for a bit more still.

COGHLAN: Well, I was going to go back to work, because, you know, I need the money now.

ARCHER: Yeah, of course.

COGHLAN: I've had my phone changed.

ARCHER: Well done, well done. And I'm sorry you have been through all this inconvenience

COGHLAN: Well, I just, I thought if I went away altogether then nobody could get to me. But according to my neighbours,

Below: *Monica Coghlan, the prostitute at the centre of the scandal, on holiday in Spain with her young son.*

'I AM JUST TRYING TO HELP YOU. GET HIS NAME AND I WILL GET HIM OFF YOUR BACK'

they're there every day.

ARCHER: I'm surprised. I thought they weren't. But if you say nothing – I admit they will try to trick you – but if you say nothing they can't...

COGHLAN: But I mean, can't you do anything for me?

ARCHER: Yes I will. Now I've got the man's name I can do something. K-U-R-T-H-A. I will do everything in my power to see that he doesn't bother you again. You are being very brave and I admire you.

TAPE D: Extracts from their telephone conversation on 23 October 1986 – the second telephone call.

COGHLAN: Hi, did you...

ARCHER: Yes I did. I got a real grip of it today. Did you go to Tunisia on holiday?

COGHLAN: To Djerba...

ARCHER: Do you, I mean do you have friends out there?

COGHLAN: I just took a holiday.

ARCHER: Well, I am sorry for what you're going through. They may still try to talk to you but I have done two things today which will frighten them.

COGHLAN: What's that?

ARCHER: I can't tell you but I can assure you that it's been done.

COGHLAN: I just want these people off my back.

ARCHER: Well, that's what I worked on today.

COGHLAN: You're telling me that you have done something today, you're not telling me what.

ARCHER: Well, I have spoken to two newspapers as well. Do you want to go abroad again?

COGHLAN: Go abroad again?

ARCHER: Uhm...

COGHLAN: Well, it'd make things easier for me, of course.

ARCHER: What I'm saying is, if a friend of mine helped you...

COGHLAN: A friend of yours...?

ARCHER: ...helped you financially to go abroad again, would that interest you?

COGHLAN: Well, look, I'm not trying to hassle you.

ARCHER: Debbie, I realise that.

COGHLAN: I'm a prostitute, that's how I earn my living. I'm very good at it, right?

ARCHER: Right.

COGHLAN: If by me going on holiday

again you could get things sorted out in between or whatever, yes, I would do that. This has taken me, you know, since this happened with you and I, it's been seven weeks and for them seven weeks I've just, you know, things... I just can't go back home.

ARCHER: I understand what you're saying Debbie, I'm trying to help you.

COGHLAN: You sending me away for two more weeks, what difference is that going to make? I need some guarantees.

ARCHER: I can't guarantee that, hard as I am trying to do my end. Well, I'm telling, I'm saying now if a friend of mine supplied some money for you to go abroad...

COGHLAN: Who is the friend?

ARCHER: Well, it doesn't matter. He'd come and give you the money and that's

Above: *Robert Alexander QC, the brilliant lawyer for Jeffrey Archer. His penetrating questions and unstinting quest for truth won the day.*

'THEY MAY STILL TRY TO TALK TO YOU BUT I HAVE DONE TWO THINGS TODAY WHICH WILL FRIGHTEN THEM'

that...

COGHLAN: I think you know what a person I am. I know that you've met me, right, and you know that I looked after you, there was no hassle of anything like that. You know that guy told me that day we was going in, he told me who you was and if I really wanted it out for you I would have looked for different distinguishing marks or whatever, but I didn't...

ARCHER: Debbie, I know...

COGHLAN: As far as I'm concerned, I've sacrificed what I have for you, right. I've not asked you really to do anything for me.

ARCHER: I accept that totally.

COGHLAN: It's Kurtha that really worries me.

ARCHER: Well, I will tell you after today he will be a very frightened man.

COGHLAN: All right, you say you're going to sort it out or you can deal with people.

ARCHER: Where will you be tomorrow?

COGHLAN: The station.

ARCHER: My friend will never find you...

COGHLAN: I just feel scared...

ARCHER: He'll just pass you an envelope and go away.

COGHLAN: You must know somewhere in Victoria?

ARCHER: Some part of Victoria Station... the number, a platform on Victoria Station would be easy.

COGHLAN: A platform...

ARCHER: Platform number three.

COGHLAN: What, on the station or the underground?

ARCHER: No, the station.

COGHLAN: ...the entrance.

ARCHER: At 11 o'clock.

COGHLAN: Well, how will he know me?

ARCHER: You'll be standing there.

COGHLAN: I'll have a green...

ARCHER: ...leather suit?

COGHLAN: Yeah.

ARCHER: Now, how long do you think you can stay abroad?

COGHLAN: Well, if you tell me, you know, you tell me what you want me to do.

ARCHER: Right. Well, if you'll tell me from abroad and tell me you've got there safely, and when you ring on this phone please don't ever speak to anyone else.

After such electrifying recordings, playing in the serene calm of the court, pressmen

and observers alike began to get an idea of the plot that had taken place around Archer. Monica Coghlan, a street prostitute, had been in the pay and protection of *The News of the World* and was ringing up Jeffrey Archer in a bid to get him to admit that he had slept with her – something he never did. Instead, in a show of charm and courtesy, he offered to help her away from the man Kurtha who had obviously, it seemed to him, been blabbing all over London his lies that he had seen him with her.

Mr. Alexander told the jury that the whole background of the conversation was one in which Archer was determined to clear his name. But he admitted that it had been a mistake for him to offer the prostitute money. 'That was clearly, looking back on it, a very foolish thing to do,' said Alexander. 'Because it was easy to be misconstrued by those who wished to misconstrue it.' He said Archer had been taking Coghlan at face value and had been trying to stop a very wicked story being circulated about him. He also thought he could help her out of trouble. In referring to the *Star* story – the crux of the case, not *The News of the World* one – he said: 'The story sought to totally destroy Mr. Archer's career. They were saying that Mr. Archer would have sex with a prostitute whose speciality was perversion.'

IN THE WITNESS BOX

On that same first day Mr. Archer stepped into the witness box to give his reasons why he had paid money to someone he had never met. He said: 'It's not unusual for me to receive lots of calls from people who cannot handle their life, or who say that there is something wrong with their life. So it was not a total surprise when something like this happens.

'It did worry me if someone was going around London saying that I had had a relationship with a prostitute. It struck me I should find out who this person was and the only way I could do this was if the person who had phoned me was to tell it to me. She had said that she would find the name and address of the person spreading these stories. I confess to not having taken it wholly seriously and assumed that if she saw the police it would die because there was no truth in it.'

JEFFREY ARCHER ADMITTED THAT IT HAD BEEN A MISTAKE FOR HIM TO OFFER THE PROSTITUTE MONEY

Above: *Mrs Mary Archer leaves the High Court after another gruelling day of testimony.*

It was assumed that on such an electrifying first day that any testimony to follow would by nature be mundane. But on Friday 10 July Monica Coghlan, perhaps the real star of this show, wearing a light grey suit and white shirt, appeared in court, pointed nervously from the witness stand towards Mr. Archer, and unwaveringly said: 'That's him'.

Asking her about the night of 8 September the previous year, when she is alleged to have had sex with Mr. Archer, the *Star*'s QC Mr. Michael Hill told her to detail what happened. She said she went into a hotel with a client, London solicitor Aziz Kurtha. Afterwards, outside the hotel, she claimed Kurtha saw her talking to a man. 'He told me that it was Jeffrey Archer, the well-known author, and he said something about him being an MP,' said Monica.

A TAWDRY MATTER

Later, she said she and Archer went into room 6A of the Albion Hotel where they had sex at an agreed rate of £50. She told the hushed courtroom: 'I told him if he took some time and I took my time and made it a bit longer it would be another £20. He agreed and gave me another £20 note. Then he got undressed. He commented on how lovely I was.' She said sex took about ten minutes. 'Because it was over so quickly I suggested that he relax for a while and then we could try again,' she said.

Former Cambridge don Mrs. Archer did not look at her nemesis when she took the witness stand, but she did take copious notes of what she had said. At one stage, there was a famous quote from Monica Coghlan that she remembered that her client had had a 'spotty back'. And, later on in the trial, in an equally famous quote, Mrs. Archer defiantly said that her husband's back was quite free from blemish.

In the end, after two weeks of evidence, it emerged that only the story told by Mr. Archer was the genuine one. His claim that he was having dinner at the exclusive Le Caprice restaurant on the night of his alleged sexual encounter was corroborated by his dinner partner and no witnesses provided by the *Star*, including *The News of the World* team which had actually set up the bugged telephone calls, could prove that he had slept with Monica Coghlan.

It was easy by the end of the case to see which side the Judge was coming down on. He made a memorable summing up, one in which he referred to the 'fragrance' of Mary Archer, and one clearly designed to leave the jury in no doubts about where he stood in the whole tawdry matter. The jury saw it his way too, and when they filed back into the court a little after two hours, Mr. Michael Hill breathed into the ear of *Star* editor Mr. Turner and said: 'We've lost'.

It was the size of the loss that stunned the *Star* – the biggest libel damages in history, plus costs, which boosted the bill to something approaching £800,000. Outside the court Jeffrey Archer emerged with his wife Mary into a sea of supporters and pressmen, clamouring for a shot of the victor.

His reputation had emerged intact in the nastiest brush with chequebook journalism in many a long year. Now Lord Archer, he can look back on the case as one that was worth fighting, no matter the agony at the time.

> IT WAS EASY BY THE END OF THE CASE TO SEE WHICH SIDE THE JUDGE WAS GOING TO COME DOWN ON

Below: *Jeffrey Archer, vindicated. It had been an emotional roller-coaster, but he had won back his good name.*

DUKE OF DRUGS
Jamie Blandford

Many wealthy people have dabbled in drugs at one time or another. But the Marquess of Blandford went a step further and became a fully-fledged junkie. That eventually led to the man who was heir to a vast estate being confined to a prison cell.

The noble Marlborough family has produced many fine Englishmen during its time. The 8th Duke of Marlborough, for example, was a hero of empire during the latter half of the 19th century; and Winston Leonard Spencer Churchill was a cousin of the Marlborough clan who became Britain's saviour in World War Two. The Marlborough family was one of immense wealth and privilege, Englishmen who put duty before self and honour above everything.

In fact, there are two-and-a-half whole pages about the family in Debrett's Peerage, the bible of the aristocracy in Britain. But perhaps there was something in the family motto which betrayed an underlying misery, a clue perhaps to the tormented nature of the tribe which was a bedfellow to its privilege and wealth. 'Faithful Though Unfortunate' is the motto – and nowhere does it apply more accurately than to the Marquess of Blandford, commonly known as the Junkie Earl in tabloid headlines.

Nowhere in British society is there to be found a more striking portrait of a man who truly had everything... only to be brought down to the gutter by that great leveller of modern day society; drugs. Jamie Blandford is a parable for our times.

The medieval philosopher Francis Bacon wrote: 'As for nobility in particular persons, it is a reverend thing to see an ancient castle or building not in decay; or to see a fair timber tree sound and perfect. How

Opposite: *Jamie Blandford has squandered a fortune and his family name through his drug addiction.*

Below: *The splendid family home, Blenheim Palace, symbol of wealth and good breeding.*

oldest and most respected families. He was born on 24 November 1955 to the then 29-year-old Marquess of Blandford – the current Duke of Marlborough – and his first wife Susan Hornby, of the W.H. Smith bookshop family. His was an aristocratic birth, childhood and upbringing – everything tailored for his unique – and most would say enviable – position in life.

CHILDHOOD TRAUMA

Blandford's parents divorced when he was five. Jamie, as he was universally known both then and now, seemed to have weathered the break-up badly; he fell back in later life to blaming the childhood trauma of divorce for some of his mammoth problems. But there were those who believe that it affected him more deeply than even he knew. The English gift for a stiff upper lip in the face of adversity can be a double-edged sword – it also stifles emotions and feelings that would best be gotten rid of through expression. Blandford would later recall the time he said goodbye to his father when he went to live with his mother in the Oxfordshire village of Little Coxwell: 'He drove me to prep school and I remember distinctly leaning over the side of the car to kiss him goodbye. But he said: "No, no, no – we don't do that anymore." The conse-

Above: *Jamie's father cutting a celebration cake with his bride, Tina Livanos, in 1961.*

Right: *Sir Winston Churchill, whose family is related to the Blandfords.*

much more to behold an ancient noble family, which hath stood against the waves and weathers of time!' The Marlborough clan undoubtedly wished it were the case with them. But the ravages of 20th century pursuits, particularly that of drug addiction, have brought sorrow to the ramparts of their stately homes.

Charles James Spencer-Churchill, the Marquess of Blandford, is in line to inherit the title of 12th Duke of Marlborough. He also becomes the Earl of Sunderland, Earl of Marlborough, Baron Spencer, Baron Churchill of Sandridge, a prince of the Holy Roman Empire as well as Prince of Mindelheim in Swabia. With those titles comes a fortune in the region of £100,000,000, a seat in the House of Lords, Blenheim Palace, 12,000 acres of land and the historical luggage of one of Britain's

quence of this was fear of rejection, which from then onwards, up to this very present day, scarred my mind. And that's why the relationship as such between us has broken down. I don't blame my father – that's how it was in those days. He, in turn, was brought up by my grandmother with a rod of iron – literally.'

At Harrow, the public school attended by so many of England's statesmen and aristocrats – including his cousin Sir Winston – he was an unremarkable pupil who nonetheless is remembered as cheerful and adept at athletics. His former master Geoffrey Treasure said: 'It's sad what became of him, but it didn't have to be so. There was never any question of him being removed from the school. I think his problem later on was through having a very difficult home life. Certainly the impression I got was that he was rather out on a limb – not at school, though; at school he was gregarious and happy.'

There was a famous occasion that his schoolchum Harry Baden-Powell, a fellow member of the school's cross country running team, well remembers. He said: 'When addressed by a bossy schoolmaster one day he is rumoured to have replied: "You can't tell me what to do – I am going to be the Duke of Marlborough." I think he understood that school rules were pretty irrelevant for someone who is worth more practically than everybody else put together.'

ARISTOCRATIC CONFUSION

At 18, dashingly handsome and eminently suitable for marriage, Jamie Blandford was headlined in the newspapers as the most eligible bachelor in the kingdom. But like Prince Charles, he suffered from a lack of sense of purpose and direction. He knew that the glittering prizes of an aristocratic birth were always there waiting for him and they seemed somehow to weigh him down more than spur him on. He has said in interviews: 'I do feel confused about my destiny and I have always resented having my life mapped out for me. I really don't know what to do with my life...'

As a young man on the threshold of adulthood, he tried many things. He enrolled at the Royal Agricultural College in Cirencester for a brief period, intent on studying farming with a view to devoting his life to becoming a gentleman landowner. He later went to Australia to herd sheep on a cattle ranch in the outback, an experience that he thoroughly enjoyed for a short while. Upon his return he tried to get into the army, but failed, and pulled strings on the old boy network from Harrow to get a job in the City of London as an insurer. The City offers magnificent opportunities to men as well connected as the Marquess, but there was something lacking in the character of Jamie Blandford; something which made him reject the disciplines of hard work and conformity. As if living up to the family motto, he truly became unfortunate.

He plunged into society life in London, a heady world of endless socialising and massive alcohol intake. But soon that wasn't enough for him; he craved satisfaction in something else – and found it in drugs. From marijuana, to cocaine to –

He plunged into society life in London — a heady world of endless socialising and massive alcohol intake

Below: *The boater-hatted boys of Harrow. Even such a privileged beginning as this was not sufficient to keep Jamie Blandford upon the straight and narrow in life.*

lected driving offences the way some people collect stamps; once he had the dubious distinction of being banned twice in one week. Always there were the sage comments from the bench about a misspent life, the waste of talent and privilege, the comments that he had been dealt every advantage in life, and yet had managed to turn them all into the most appalling burdens. There did, indeed, seem to be no end to his downward spiral.

worst of all – heroin, he tried to seek new experiences. All these drugs were taken along with copious amounts of booze. At the peak of his drug problem in the early 1980s he was spending up to £1,500 a week on drugs – drugs which he hid in toilet cisterns, cocktail cabinets and under stairways as he tried to maintain the facade of a 'casual' user: one who handled drugs in social settings only. In reality, he was a slave to the mind-bending drugs and it is necessary in this chronicle to give just the briefest details of his descent into hell.

Both his father and his late stepsister Christina Onassis, of the hugely wealthy Onassis clan, tried to force him into rehabilitation clinics when they realised that the drugs had completely taken over his life. They paid for him to enter an expensive £1,000 a day Parisian clinic – which he escaped from by breaking out of a window. At another clinic he burned down a potting shed. Back on the streets he was prey to the dealers and the scumbags once more.

PROBATION AND PRISON

It was inevitable that such a degrading lifestyle would run headlong into the path of the law. In 1985, Blandford was fined and put on probation for breaking into a chemist's in his desperate search for drugs. Within six months he was in court again, then sentenced to three months in prison. In 1986, he was released, only to receive another suspended sentence for the possession of cocaine. On top of all this he col-

Above Left and Above: *The world of the junkie is a depraved, dispiriting one, where the 'fix' is the only priority in each waking hour. It has led Jamie Blandford to ruin.*

But in 1987 he met a beautiful, understanding and loving woman named Rebecca Few Brown, a blueblood who counted the Duchess of York among her friends. Rebecca had a stabilising influence upon him. She selflessly devoted herself to trying to help him conquer his appalling addictions. Like Princess Diana, she was a kindergarten teacher before she found herself in the unwelcome spotlight of publicity; unlike Diana, she was the target of newspaper cameramen and reporters because of her relationship with a junkie, not the heir to the throne of England.

She was not on the same social scale as Blandford, but she was acceptably 'society' enough to be known on the circuit in London and the Home Counties. One of her former classmates at the Hampden House School in Great Missenden, Buckinghamshire, was Antonia de Sancha, the sometime actress who would later find infamy from her relationship with the Tory cabinet minister David Mellor.

'Rebecca was pleasant enough,' recalled a friend, 'but she got pushed around a bit. She was a bit pathetic. The school was not the kind to turn out brain surgeons and High Court judges – and in that she did not disappoint. Our school, basically, was filled with its share of rich thickos from broken homes in the shires.'

Ski-mad Becky took to the slopes of the swish European alpine resorts where 'the set' routinely holidayed during the winter season. She went into business with friend Cess Morrison, catering for ski-parties with wholesome food and plenty of fine wines. At one stage she was feeding former world motor racing champion Jackie Stewart at his luxury villa overlooking Lake Geneva in Switzerland where Prince Philip was an occasional visitor.

Her first proper relationship was with Princess Margaret's friend Ben Holland-Martin, and it was he who first brought her to the chalet called The Gay Gnomes, owned by Paddy McNally, the sometime racing entrepreneur who was romantically linked with Fergie for some time before her romance with Prince Andrew.

BACHELOR PARTY

Before meeting Blandford, Rebecca had a fling with McNally as he sought solace over the break-up with Fergie. The relationship was bumpy – he was, after all, old enough to be her father – and while she was looking for something permanent, insiders in the set say he was merely enjoying a fling. When they finally split, bachelor girl Becky met bachelor Blandford at a party during one of his less crazy periods and he became spellbound by her. A friend at the time told noted author and journalist Christopher Wilson: 'Jamie became obsessed with her, like he did with all his women. They got together, broke up, got together, broke up – it was that sort of rela-

tionship. The minute she said she didn't want to know him any more, Jamie decided that's when he wanted to marry her and that's when he popped the question.'

The wedding was in 1990. A healthy, beaming Marquess of Blandford appeared in the newspaper looking nothing like the shell of a few years earlier when his most famous appearances had been behind a mahogany rail in magistrates' courts. The nation rejoiced, too, in his marriage; the British do not like to see a man down forever. But the same cannot be said of his rigid, austere father, who, it is believed, was angry that his son had married beneath him. He was also said to be upset at the choice of best man – none other than Paddy McNally, Rebecca's former lover. McNally gave the newlyweds a top-of-the-line Range Rover car, worth over £35,000. One guest observed drily: 'It was almost a thank

AT HIS WEDDING, BLANDFORD LOOKED NOTHING LIKE THE SHELL OF A FEW YEARS EARLIER

Below: *Jamie Blandford walks in a London street shortly after one of his cocaine suppliers was jailed.*

Above: *Jamie as a cheeky five-year-old pageboy at a 1961 wedding.*

A YEAR AFTER THE MARRIAGE, BLANDFORD AGAIN FOUND HIMSELF BACK BEHIND BARS — FOR DRIVING WHILE BANNED

you for Jamie for taking Becky off of his hands. It was frankly way over the top. We all looked in the opposite direction.'

But while she had achieved miracles in turning Blandford around from his drugs self-destruction, there was already trouble in the marriage before the honeymoon was over. Rows were witnessed in hotel corridors by guests in San Tropez. On one occasion, Rebecca was seen in tears as a result of her husband's verbal bullying. Upon their return to Britain they moved into The Lince, a beautiful Georgian House on the Blenheim Estate that Blandford is one day destined to inherit. Nearby, an army of workmen toiled around the clock to carry out improvements to the £1,000,000 Wooton Down Farm, the 12-bedroomed Cotswold farmhouse set on 850 acres of prime land that his father was giving to him as a wedding present. A year after the marriage, Blandford was back behind bars, serving 37 days of a three-month jail sen-

tence for driving while banned. Six months after that a son, named George, was born to the happy couple and friends once again presumed that the daughter of a chartered surveyor had done what the finest public schools of England and all the wealth and privilege that was his birthright could not: reform a weak character who was incapable of reforming himself.

IN TROUBLE AGAIN

The happy pictures of Blandford and Becky with their newborn son, however, were papering over the cracks in a crumbling facade. Behind her back, Blandford had plunged into the partying piranha pool again. He had also taken London apartments for the purposes of entertaining women and was soon back where he had started. Three years after they had married they separated, and Blandford was once again in trouble. In January 1993 there was the most extraordinary attack on Blandford by Lord Spencer-Churchill, his uncle, who told of how exasperated everyone who was ever close to Jamie had become, including his own father who knew that one day he was obliged to pass on the magnificent estate and lands to him.

He said: 'All I know is that without having James certified mad, my brother cannot stop him inheriting the Dukedom. I don't think James is prepared to listen to anyone. He is acting like a befuddled megalomaniac. He insults people. I think he behaves despicably. I know what traumas my brother is going through. After everything my brother has done – and he has done a remarkable job at Blenheim – it must be an awful worry to him that when James inherits, everything is going to crumble.

'The family is deeply concerned for his health. It would be better for James if he seeks medical help but it seems difficult for him to realise that he needs such help. His father is deeply fond of James, as we all are. We are a very united family. I think my brother feels deeply let down by him and there has been a lot of suffering in the family. We have tried to help him out, my goodness how we have tried.'

At the time of his outburst Becky had taken George to her mother's home in Cottisford, not far from the Blenheim estate, while her estranged husband galli-

vanted around London, often with numerous pretty young things on his arm. Becky was certainly not missed by Blandford's father – she revealed how he had branded her a 'dirty little scrubber' after appearing scantily clad in the top people's magazine *Tatler*. 'Everything's your fault,' she claimed he said. 'I never want to speak to you again.'

BLANDFORD'S AGONY

Experts believed that it was the thought of responsibilities as a father which plunged Jamie off the deep end once more. As mentioned, he had a bitter childhood, in which he believed he was starved of love and attention. Dr. Sebastian Kraemer, a child psychologist at London's respected Tavistock Clinic, said: 'If you have never been loved, or have been neglected as a child, it creates a considerable obstacle when it comes to your turn to be a parent. Good parenthood is something that we learn from our own parents. Blandford's

agony at not being able to see his child will be no different to anyone else's in the same situation. It is the worst pain any father can experience, but he is quite right to blame his drug and drink dependency on his cool upbringing. Most addicts we see are like big babies – they haven't been able to grow up and accept the responsibilities of adulthood because of something missing in their childhoods. Many come from difficult backgrounds. But it is not good enough for him to just say: "Oh, well, I can behave badly because I had a difficult childhood." It's a reason, but it's not an excuse.'

A court ruling was put on Blandford early in 1993 to stop him from pestering Becky and his baby son. Lord Spencer-Churchill sided with her as friends rallied round to give her solace. He said: 'Becky has behaved like a perfect lady. I think she has conducted herself in the most exemplary, dignified way, bearing in mind the harassment she has been through. The irony is that there are some cases of people who have no money at all but are very

'HE IS QUITE RIGHT TO BLAME HIS DRUG AND DRINK DEPENDENCY ON HIS COOL UPBRINGING' happy. I think that power corrupts and money corrupts and if you don't know how to use it, and you don't know how to behave with it, this is the way you end up. But luckily the majority of people are more level-headed and more sophisticated when it comes to money and power.'

CRACK REPORTER

To show how far and how hard Blandford had fallen the Sunday newspaper, *The News of the World*, sent a reporter to gate-crash a drugs party where Jamie Blandford extolled the virtues of dealing crack on the street. It was in March 1993, and showed that, far from being on the road to recovery, he was still in the grip of the drug. The party was held at a £300,000 flat of a wealthy female friend in Chelsea – with Blandford cycling to make the rendezvous because of his driving ban. Blandford was exposed as a 'crackhead' – someone who gets high on the cheapest, most dangerous form of cocaine there is. Crack is an import from America, where whole inner city

areas have been laid waste by the drug as it has destroyed families, communities and basic human decencies. Essentially it is cocaine mixed with other ingredients into small white balls – crack rocks. These are heated by the user in a glass pipe or other smoking implement. There is a little smoke which the addict inhales for a massive, instant high. There are numerous reported cases of first-time crack users dying as the jolt from the drug hits their hearts like a kick from a mule. Those who survive become pathetic slaves to the substance – and will sink to any levels in a bid to get more and more of it.

The dossier compiled by *The News of the World* was handed to Scotland Yard, who confirmed they were investigating it. But here is part of the transcript of a taped conversation with Blandford, together with explanations of some of the drug-world terms as written by reporter Chris Blythe.

'He phoned a drug-dealing partner to complain about some undersized crack rocks they had been sold. The drug-crazed conversation, recorded on tape, went as follows: "Is the dude da? Yeah, where are you? We need to sort them things out. They're too small, them things, or we're going to lose customers. You slipped me another one of those yellow bellies." (Impure crack.) He put the phone down and retreated with the girls to a side room. Twenty minutes later they returned to the front room with bulging eyes and dilated pupils after a drug fix. Blandford – in jeans and a brown leather jacket – sat on the sofa and began jabbering intensely. He said: "As from tomorrow I'm getting some weights the size of a calculator. They're smaller than this, yeah, and they weigh to .01." (His reference to electronic scales accurate enough to measure within 0.01 of a gramme.)

'He went on: "So from tomorrow everything is going to be absolutely spot. I mean you probably lose out on stuff in the end... But I mean, what you lose out in weight you gain in customers." (The scales are so accurate it will be impossible to short-change junkies – but that will also make them trust you more.) He then spoke to the girls about our reporter and said: "Does he want to talk to me or what?"'

BLYTHE: I could definitely do some (drugs).

Below: *New Scotland Yard – hardly a fitting place for a noble to end up, but Blandford has become familiar with police stations and policemen throughout his life.*

BLANDFORD: Well, let me tell you something – the more you buy, the better the deal is. You realise that, you know.

He then began advising our reporter on the tricks of his trade. He claimed £500 would buy an ounce of crack in the shape of a disc, which had been moulded in the bottom of a cut-off Lucozade bottle. The discs are made by heating the cocaine with another substance and adding cold water so the mixture solidifies.

BLANDFORD: For 500 quid you could get a disc. Like the bottom of a Lucozade bottle.
BLYTHE: Five hundred notes?
BLANDFORD: That's an ounce. An ounce of powder washed up. If you can get it for 500, let me know where.
BLYTHE: So you're talking about a grand for that really?
BLANDFORD: Oh yeah, absolutely. You know what you've got to understand, right, is that if you buy 500 quid's worth – you cut it, you should be able to make 500 on top.
(By cutting it he meant either breaking a crack disc into rocks or diluting cocaine by mixing it with another white powder.)

BLYTHE: You reckon?
BLANDFORD: Certainly 250.
BLYTHE: Well, that's reasonable in that case.

In further drug conversations Blandford smoked crack through a biro pen case, introduced the reporter to a drug-dealer who handed over £280 worth of crack-cocaine to him and spoke about how the 'sensible people' smoke 'within their capabilities.' The crack that Blythe purchased was analysed by chemist Jeremy Wooten at a laboratory in South-East London where he declared: 'It is reasonably pure cocaine. We shall pass this to the relevant authorities.'

Scotland Yard acted on Blythe's dossier and the chemical report to stage a series of raids on a housing estate in London where several crack dealers were arrested. Blandford was not arrested and there were no legal complaints either to the newspaper or to the Press Complaints Commission. Blandford remained at large, a rebel without a cause. In May 1993 he was arrested and thrown in jail for failing to pay Becky thousands of pounds in maintenance money. He was released on appeal. His liberty was probably fleeting.

'WITH BULGING EYES AND DILATED PUPILS AFTER A DRUG FIX, BLANDFORD SAT ON THE SOFA AND BEGAN JABBERING INTENSELY'

BLANDFORD SMOKED CRACK THROUGH A BIRO PEN CASE AND INTRODUCED THE REPORTER TO A DRUG DEALER

Below: *It appears to be too much for Jamie Blandford as he leaves yet another court after yet another appearance.*

MONACO MADNESS
The House of Grimaldi

Prince Rainier and Princess Grace of Monaco were universally regarded as royalty's most distinguished couple. But when their three children began looking for independence, the dignity of the House of Grimaldi soon became seriously threatened.

Monte Carlo; the very name conjures up nights of elegance and excess. Fortunes gambled on the casino tables, beautiful women on the sun-kissed beaches, a walk on the elegant corniche before dinner at any one of a hundred elegant and fabulously expensive restaurants. Monte Carlo is the main city of Monaco,

the 12th century principality which, along with Liechtenstein and Andorra, has remained time-locked in a Europe which has seen vast change.

Monaco has a ruling royal family called Grimaldi, which was saved from decay and maybe even extinction by the marriage of its ruler, Prince Rainier, to the glamorous Hollywood actress Grace Kelly in the 1950s. The marriage of the potentate to the

Opposite: *Prince Rainier of Monaco (standing centre) on the 25th anniversary of his reign, with (clockwise from top right) Prince Albert, and Princesses Stephanie, Grace and Caroline.*

Below: *Monaco – home to roulette wheels and yachts.*

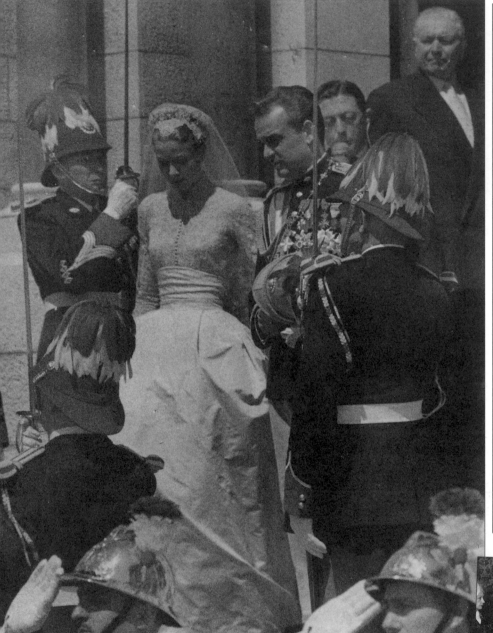

Princess Caroline was the golden child, the first born into the new dynasty, on 23 January 1957. Grace Kelly had arrived just the previous year and the birth of a girl into the old dynasty was celebrated throughout the world. 'All seemed under control,' wrote a newspaper, 'until the children started to grow up.' Princess Caroline had an upbringing where she wanted for nothing. A sheltered education in the palace under the tutelage of governesses was followed by several terms at the dignified St. Mary's girls' school in Ascot. She was a distinguished scholar whose beauty was apparent at a very early age.

THE TOPLESS PRINCESS

But she was guaranteed a place in the scandal hall of fame – and an eternal following of photographers around the world – when she became, at 21, the first princess ever pictured topless. It was at the Monte Carlo Beach Club, haunt of much of Europe's rich, handsome and famous, and it sent her parents into a frenzy of anger. They tried confining her to the palace. They tried cutting off her allowance. But Caroline was a girl whose will was not to be tamed. She had begun, shortly after her topless episode at the beach club, an affair with French playboy Philippe Junot. Her parents strong-

actress turned Monaco into a veritable Disneyworld-sur-mer and the spotlight has rarely been off of this tax-free paradise ever since.

But the royal children spawned in the marriage between Rainier and Princess Grace have frequently failed to give the ruler the kind of solace that he would have liked to have found in his autumn years. The Princesses Caroline and Stephanie, and the heir Prince Albert, have led lives rich in scandal, embarrassment and personal tragedy. It's no wonder that Prince Rainier is often referred to as 'Grey Head' by his citizens – the antics of his children have done little for his nerves or his hair colour!

Above: *The fairy tale begins – the wedding of movie star Grace Kelly to Prince Rainier in 1956. She would give celebrity status to the backwater monarchy of Europe.*

Right: *The couple sit solemnly in the throne room of the palace in Monaco before exchanging vows.*

Left: *Prince Rainier and Grace, flanked by Albert and Caroline, attend a Red Cross Ball in Monaco.*

Below: *Princess Caroline and Philippe Junot in Monaco after their 1978 wedding.*

ly disapproved of the liaison and did their best to keep them apart. Ultimately, because she had reached the age at which she did not need parental consent to strike out on her own, she decided to marry him, with or without their consent.

There was a full state wedding in 1978 to Junot, but the marriage was doomed from the start. Princess Caroline, back from her cruising honeymoon off the French Riviera, found out that her playboy catch had actually made approaches to the more lurid publications of Europe in a bid to sell topless poses of his new bride that he had snapped on honeymoon. In her grief she confided to her mother – a woman who had always been appalled by him.

'Leave him or marry him,' her mother had said when Caroline, before the nuptials, had railed at her domineering mama's dislike of her lover. 'I did it to spite mama,' she later told friends with regard to her decision to marry Junot. 'It was a very bad mistake.' The marriage lasted precisely 831 days, although relations between the two had been destroyed long before the end.

The divorce was a painful affair to Prince Rainier because of the staunch Catholicism in his family. Caroline applied for a Papal annulment to the marriage, which was eventually delivered 12 years later. Junot later complained that it was

Prince Rainier and his wife who had driven the wedge between him and his bride. He said: 'They did everything in their power to avoid our being alone, even for a minute. I was given no opportunity to sort out our problems as any other couple would have been able to do. Caroline was taken away from me, our home in Paris locked up and all communication, even by telephone, was made impossible. All this created a deep well of bitterness inside me which took years to overcome. Perhaps we had life too easy… we saw each other within a sort of cyclone which made our lives go round so quickly, and ultimately made us unhappy.'

THE PREGNANT BRIDE

Caroline, however, found both happiness – and pregnancy – within what some say was an indecently short time after she broke up with Junot. She met and fell in love with the son of an Italian industrialist named Stefano Casiraghi and she was pregnant when she married him in a civil ceremony in 1981. Caroline was deeply hopeful that her children would be recognised by the Catholic church – which was rather doubtful, because the offspring of a divorced woman in the faith are usually deemed illegitimate. 'I put my trust in the church's charity,' said Caroline, although it would be many years before the kind of charity she was seeking would be forthcoming.

Above: *Caroline looks blissfully happy upon her engagement to Italian businessman Stefano Casiraghi.*

Right: *The couple evade the cameramen as they speed off for a romantic holiday before their wedding.*

Opposite: *The beautiful Princess Stephanie on a trip to New York to promote her album.*

Her friends say that the marriage was not a passionate one. Casiraghi had a long affair throughout it, with the daughter of a famous European aristocrat, and he certainly had troubles of another kind: massive debts. He became a construction magnate in Monte Carlo, reclaiming land from the sea for further development in the cramped principality. He also owned yachts and a helicopter service, with 12 craft, each costing £1,500,000. But it was a house built on sand – the empire was owned by banks who loaned him the money and they came calling for their cash. Caroline was forced to put up £1,000,000 worth of her late mother's jewels as collateral to the banks to stop them foreclosing on his businesses.

Shrewdly she contacted an old flame, Roberto Rossellini, son of Ingrid Bergman, who worked on Wall Street and asked him for the best way to salvage what was left of her husband's dwindling empire. But as she became more and more involved in his business enterprises she was seen less and less in Monaco: locals grumbled that her absence cost them 50 per cent in tourist revenues in one year, a massive amount as there is no income tax in Monaco and the tourist cash is all-important. She spent more and more time in France, enrolling her children in schools instead of frittering her time away at balls and the Grand Prix.

SPEEDBOATING TRAGEDY

In 1990, however, the sympathy of the world reached out to Caroline with the loss of Casiraghi in a speedboating accident. Eight years earlier she had earned global condolences for the death of her mother in the car crash; now she was experiencing the full weight of grief once more. She took to wearing black, lost 25lbs – at one time it was suspected she was suffering an eating disorder – and retreated from public life. It was to be almost two years before she found happiness again with Vincent Lindon, a French actor who she met at a discreet dinner party at the chateau home of an aristocratic count.

Lindon, 31, was shy, sensitive and self-effacing – a dramatic difference to the playboy types that Caroline had traditionally found herself falling for. A former lover of the daughter of French prime minister Jacques Chirac, Lindon is the son of a rich

engulf her, particularly after she moved to America where she tried to become an actress and singer. The lovechild which she was to have by her bodyguard in 1992 was said to have aged Prince Rainier by another 20 years overnight. Time will tell whether she will yet mature into a dignified, graceful beauty like her elder sister.

Stephanie was in the car that day her mother ran off the road and many say the deep scars have never totally healed. Those looking for a reason to explain her wayward behaviour have been fond of quoting that as a possible explanation for some of her more extravagant mistakes. Whatever the reason, Stephanie still seems intent on going her own way, no matter what her father or the world may think of her. The most widely photographed young woman in the world next to Princess Diana, she still commands centre stage wherever she might be.

As a child there was intense rivalry between Caroline and Stephanie. Certainly Caroline was blessed with the more classic looks of her mother while Stephanie's square jaw and masculine shoulders marked her out as a tomboy during her teens.

industrialist who may yet end up taking Caroline down the aisle a third time. It could also be a church wedding again, as the Vatican granted her an annulment for the marriage to Junot, decreeing that the marriage never existed. But Lindon has been told by Prince Rainier that he will inherit no titles and have little access to her children should the marriage end in divorce. It is yet to be seen whether those are conditions he wishes to abide by.

SEXY STEPHANIE

If Princess Caroline was a headache to her father, then Stephanie was a living nightmare. Beautiful, sensuous, she was a child of her age who cared little for the pomp and circumstance of her regal birth. With an allowance topping out at over £30,000 a month, the fleshpots of the world were hers to enjoy. Scandal after scandal seemed to

Insiders say Caroline teased her constantly, leading the younger princess to become ever more impish and impudent in her behaviour. Princess Grace once remarked of her: 'I gave up punishing her when she was only seven. I could have hit her like a gong and it wouldn't have done her any good! She got very bossy and exhausted a long line of nannies in her time.'

Unlike university-educated Caroline, Stephanie barely made it through a strict Roman Catholic high school. She was almost expelled once for putting frogs underneath the wimples of the nuns who taught her! But it was when she reached 18 and the boyish looks had given way to a taut, shapely sexiness that made her a top fashion model, that the trouble really began.

REBEL BELLE

Soon newspapers all over the world were splashed with photos of Stephanie exasperating society or the authorities wherever she happened to be. She was topless on beaches where it wasn't allowed; she was in the arms of men that her father deemed to be beneath her; she was seen lurching from all-night discotheques, the accumulated effects of too much champagne and too little sleep showing clearly upon her face.

That she was a very independent woman became clear to her father after she moved to America semi-permanently in 1988. A paparazzi photographer snapped her at a chemist's in Hollywood as she bought dozens of contraceptives!

There was a furious missive that followed from her father, threatening to cut her allowance, but Stephanie ignored it. She had recently broken up with Anthony Delon, son of the heartthrob French film actor Alain Delon, lived briefly with a playboy called Mario Olivier – who had a criminal record for sexual battery – and had taken up with Ron Bloom, a Jewish record producer who was working furiously to make her a star.

The man's religion was as much a bugbear to the Prince back home in Monaco as anything else. The House of Rainier is a strictly Catholic dynasty with rigid rules about the offspring of the principality's partners. Rainier is certainly not anti-semitic but he was adamant that she should settle down with a European blueblood.

A PAPARAZZI PHOTOGRAPHER SNAPPED HER IN HOLLYWOOD AS SHE BOUGHT DOZENS OF CONTRACEPTIVES!

Opposite Top: *Happier, more innocent days. Caroline (left) and Stephanie having fun during a 1977 skiing holiday in Switzerland.*

Opposite Bottom: *Stephanie in Los Angeles, where she increasingly spent more time during the 1980s.*

Below: *A guard of honour at Stefano Casiraghi's funeral after his death in a powerboating accident.*

Above: *Comforted by her father, Caroline pays her respects to her husband at his funeral.*

STEPHANIE GAVE LEFUR £40,000 WORTH OF PERSONAL GIFTS AND SPENT £5,000 ON HIM AT FLASHY RESTAURANTS ALL OVER EUROPE

But there was to be no permanent romance with Bloom. From him Stephanie moved on to movie star Rob Lowe – whose videotaped sex romps with an under-age schoolgirl in a hotel room in Atlanta sent the Prince into further paroxysms of anger!

In 1990, however, Stephanie took up with a man with a very dubious past – something far more sinister than someone who took sexy videos of himself performing in the bedroom. Jean-Yves Lefur was a smooth-talking French businessman who swept her off her feet after they met at a Parisian ball. Here was someone that the ultra-conservative Prince Rainier definitely approved of.

But Lefur, 27 at the time, had a secret past. In 1985 he was prisoner no. 2567843 at Fleury-Merogis prison outside of Paris where he was doing time for business fraud. Far from being a blueblood, he was the son of a man who lived in a council house who earned a living fitting out butcher shops in the capital.

It was Prince Rainier who eventually came to the rescue of Stephanie as he saw her frittering away a fortune on him. She paid the £2,500 a month on a Paris apartment they shared together. She paid for a £35,000 engagement party in Paris at the height of their love affair. She gave him £40,000 worth of personal gifts and spent £5,000 on him at flashy restaurants all over Europe.

DETECTIVE WORK PAYS OFF

Prince Rainier decided to get private detectives to run a background check on the man leeching off her daughter – and when confronted with the evidence that she had been duped she kissed him and said: 'Thank you, papa. I loved him so much I would have married him. Now I never want to hear his name mentioned again.'

After she broke up with him Stephanie plunged back into the world of singing, trying to revive a career that had never gone anywhere. But in 1992 she found herself booed off stage in Belgium by concert goers who winced at her voice. A planned South American tour was cancelled because of pathetic ticket sales. And her album *Stephanie* performed so miserably in France her record company refused to

going bad when his daughter was snapped in a sensational series of photographs, naked around a pool, cavorting with a man named Daniel Ducruet, the man hired to be her bodyguard.

Ducruet, 33, was a former Monaco policeman that Prince Rainier dubbed 'street trash' after he learned that he was doing more than merely protecting his daughter. And he hit the royal rafters when the double blow landed – one that his daughter was pregnant by him; the second that he had dumped his own girlfriend Martine Malbouvier, who had a four month old son by him, to join Stephanie's million-dollar lifestyle.

Left: *Grace the beautiful – her daughters inherited her amazing looks.*

Below: *As she is remembered by the world, a study in glamour and elegance before her untimely death.*

allow it to be released in England. 'I am not surprised that this album hasn't sold,' said Pierre Louis Berlatier, a Sony Music official in charge of promoting Stephanie's album sales in France. 'She is very nice but it would be a good idea for her to try acting instead.'

Stephanie hoped to become the next Madonna. One of her albums, *Hurricane*, had sold more than five million copies in France five years previously. But record moguls didn't have the heart to tell her that it was so popular because it was a curiosity item – bought because of who she was, not what she could do. Jerry Greenberg, a Sony Music spokesman in Los Angeles admitted that Stephanie was a total flop in America, saying: 'It just didn't happen. It went totally unnoticed.'

Stephanie turned once again to romance in a bid to cure the wounds of failure – but admitted that in affairs of the heart she had often been less than successful. In a rare moment of public candour she said: 'I guess I have been unlucky in love. Even if I have given my all, I haven't always gotten my share back. But I am not the first young woman to have had that experience.'

Prince Rainier hoped that the next one she fell for would be Mr. Right. In his eyes, however, he turned out to be the worst of the lot! Prince Rainier knew things were

'I hate them both,' fumed Martine, whose tragic story of betrayal made newspaper headlines around the world. 'They have ruined my life. It hurts and it hurts bad. When my baby cries I'm the only one who puts him to bed. There's no-one else to take care of him. I am just a working girl and Stephanie is rich and powerful. I only make £140 per week and it's rough to pay a babysitter on that salary but I have no choice.'

Prince Rainier is alleged to have raged to a friend: 'How could Stephanie do this to me? I have forgiven her for much of her wild behaviour, but this is too much. That baby will be no grandchild of mine. That man will never be part of this family!'

Stephanie's son was born in November 1992 amid much acrimony in the royal household. Prince Rainier immediately cut off her allowance, there was little contact between him and his daughter, and he refused to see the child. But he remains devoted to his daughter. And the depth of love between them was demonstrated by an extraordinary police operation just weeks after the child was born when Stephanie inadvertently found herself at the top of a Mafia death list.

A COCAINE DEAL

For years she had run with a crowd that bought and used massive amounts of drugs – cocaine being the favourite – which fuelled the long nights of partying and the sun-soaked yachting holidays. The police came to Stephanie and made a deal with her; she would supply information about a drugs lord in return for immunity from prosecution. Prince Rainier threw his hands up in resignation and urged his daughter to co-operate. She did – but her confessional sessions with the forces of law and order plunged her into danger.

Labri Dahmane, the ruthless cocaine baron who had initially identified Stephanie and her pals as being among his clients, was himself linked to the cocaine cartels of Colombia and Sicily's mafia. A police source leaked the Princess's name to the press and the mafia godfathers were furious. Stephanie had spilled the beans on one Giovanni Felice, a ruthless drug runner who for years had supplied the rich and powerful – including her – with their potions and powders.

Above: *Prince Rainier in London with Albert in 1968 after visiting the Post Office Tower together.*

Opposite Top: *Lady Helen Windsor, the British royal who briefly captured Albert's wandering heart.*

Opposite Bottom: *Albert and his father wave to the Monaco crowds. Caroline is next to Albert, standing behind her three children Andfrea, Pierre and Charlotte.*

> STEPHANIE RECEIVED SEVERAL THREATENING PHONE CALLS, ONE OF WHICH PROMISED HER THAT HER SON WAS TARGETED

Once the mafia knew that it was Stephanie that had informed, she became the target for assassination. Prince Rainier moved swiftly to take her and her child back under his wing. Her luxury penthouse apartment in Monaco was transformed into a fortress with gun-toting bodyguards watching over her around the clock. Six more guards were posted at Monaco's Princess Grace Hospital where she was receiving regular check-ups after the birth of her son. And a special armoured limousine was provided for her whenever she left the refuge of her apartment.

In all, 12 drug dealers were fingered on Stephanie's evidence. Nathalie Nottet, a French police spokeswoman, said: 'It is true that a certain young princess was involved in the operation and all the arrested individuals have been co-operating with the police.' Stephanie received several threatening phone calls, one of which promised her that her son was targeted, but so far both have remained healthy. But Princess Stephanie remains a constant worry to Prince Rainier – he wonders, as does the world, when the next scandal may surface to strike him.

THE HEIR AND SUCCESSOR

Prince Albert, as the male in the line, is considered to be the heir and successor to the House of Grimaldi, but his behaviour gives little solace to his father. Empty headed, he has lived his life as if it was one long champagne-soaked party. Always on his arm there have been bevies of beauties, ranging from Brooke Shields of Hollywood fame to Lady Helen Windsor to Princess Astrid of Belgium and countless minor royals in Europe. His nights were spent in clubs and casinos, his days soaking up the sun at poolsides and aboard million pound yachts floating lazily along the Côte d'Azur. The only thing he seemed to excel at was sports and at one time he was the captain of the Monaco bob sled team at the winter Olympics in 1991. His team came in 43rd and 23rd in two separate events.

Prince Rainier could tolerate his son's 'wild oats' spree, as long as it didn't bring disgrace upon the family name – but that is exactly what happened in November 1986 when Albert fell head over heels in love with American porn star Teri Weigel. Weigel, 29, has appeared in some of Hollywood's most shocking triple-X rated movies and met the debonair prince at a Monte Carlo party attended by Princess

Caroline. 'He lifted up my skirt and exposed me to Caroline,' said Weigel in a kiss-and-tell with an American magazine some years later.

'She was very shocked. Later he took me back to the apartment that he keeps solely for entertaining women and we made love. It was a great experience.' A livid Prince Rainier threatened to bring in legislation that would make Caroline and not Albert heir to the throne of Monaco, but Albert managed to convince his father that the affair was only fleeting.

Albert has been thoroughly tested by the antics of his three children during the past decade and a half. Those trials, added to the pain that was obvious to a watching world at Grace's funeral, have ensured that he has had widespread sympathy from those who have followed the goings-on at the House of Rainier during that time. Albert can only hope that, as his children reach maturity their behaviour begins to reflect their position and status as members of one of Europe's most glamorous royal families.

THE WINDSORS
Britain's Troubled Royals

A series of revelations concerning the excesses of the British royal family's private lives sickened the recession-hit British public in the early 1990s. After a century of living it up at the public's expense, the Windsors appeared to be living on borrowed time.

Her Majesty the Queen summed up 1992 in a Latin phrase; quite simply, it was her '*annus horribilis*', the year in which scandal seemed to dog the House of Windsor at every turn, culminating in the decision of the Prince and Princess of Wales to part, plunging the very future of the monarchy into doubt. But scandal is no stranger to royal households. It has been a bedfellow of the bluebloods of the British realm for as long as they have ruled. The House of Windsor certainly seems to have had more than its fair share of such torment, however, as the following delicious, decadent and debauched romps of the royals will show only too clearly!

It was the age of beauty and decadence, of languid summers and holidays by the sea. It was the *belle epoque* in France and the last fling of the old order in Britain before the conflagration of World War One would sweep away everything that was accepted as custom and practice. For the Prince of Wales it was the age of love and devilment – both fulfilled in his passions for a woman who became known as 'The Jersey Lily'.

Bertie, as he was known to his friends, was the jocular, life-loving hedonist who would later become King. His was an ordered world of game shoots and naval reviews, state banquets and informal dinner soirees amid London society. And a world where one took a wife for duty – and a mistress for pleasure. The great country houses of England have long echoed to the foot-steps of the admiral off for an assignation with the cleric's wife; the general off to meet the diplomat's betrothed. So it was for the aristocracy and royalty. The only rule of the game was that everything was known – but nothing was said.

BERTIE THE BONKER

Possessed of an enormous sexual appetite which the brothels of Europe could do little to satisfy, Bertie took to bedding the wives and mistresses of friends – and later used to regale the cuckolded husbands and lovers with tales of the pleasure he took! He lost his virginity when he was 19 to actress Nellie Clifton, while he was stationed at Curragh Military Camp outside Dublin and never looked back. Queen Victoria was most definitely not amused by her son's

Above: *Edward the Caresser, Prince of Wales, dallied with one of the most brazen women of his day.*

Opposite: *The happy family of the House of Windsor upon the marriage of Prince Charles to Lady Diana Spencer in 1981.*

LILLIE LANGTRY'S RELATIONSHIP WITH BERTIE SHATTERED THE CLAY FEET OF THE BRITISH MONARCHICAL FIGURES FOREVER

Above: *Queen Victoria at her most stern. She ruled an empire upon which the sun never set – and spawned a bloodline with roving eyes and unfaithful hearts.*

VICTORIA LOVED HER SON, BUT REMAINED CONVINCED THAT HIS SHENANIGANS HAD BROUGHT ABOUT THE DEATH OF HER BELOVED ALBERT

continuous courting of scandal, but there was very little she could do to contain him. She loved her son, but remained convinced throughout her later years that his shenanigans had brought about the death of her beloved Albert, who died in 1861. 'That boy,' she wrote. 'Much as I pity I never can, or shall, look at him without a shudder.'

PRINCE OF SCANDAL

Victoria nurtured the idea that he might change his scandalous ways with his marriage to Princess Alexandra of the royal house of Denmark in 1863, but she was to be proved sadly wrong. Although Alexandra was reared in the finest tradition of European royalty, groomed for the high office she would someday command, and was pretty, witty, intelligent and charming,

it would never be enough to satisfy the roving eye of Bertie. Soon, after a blissful honeymoon, he had slipped back to his bachelor ways – ways which included gallivanting across Europe to places like Monte Carlo and Biarritz, and bringing back an interesting selection of society friends to his London home, Marlborough House, for dinner parties, all-night card games and general debauchery.

The first taste of the scandal that was to come occurred when he was hauled into court as the witness to a gambling debt. The second was when he was named in a divorce case by Lady Harriet Mordaunt, who insisted that he was one of her many lovers. The establishment of the British monarchy rallied around Bertie, as did his family, and the case was dismissed in the end because of the unstable nature of Lady Mordaunt's mind. But it rocked Bertie and many of his fellows in society who believed he was heading for much stormier seas. The tempest occurred in the shape of Lillie Langtry, an actress and celebrated beauty of her age whose relationship with the Prince of Wales forever shattered the clay feet of the idols who were the British monarchical figures.

Lillie was born Emilie Charlotte le Breton in Jersey in 1853 to a highly sexed church official known among parishioners as the 'Dirty Dean'. It was rumoured that his dalliances had been so numerous on the island he had to break up his daughter's first puppy love affair when she was 17 – because the boy in question was a bastard who he had fathered in one of his numerous illicit dalliances.

A VOLUPTUOUS TEMPTRESS

Jersey, her father knew, would always be a place too small to contain such a beauty and firebrand as his daughter. She was voluptuous and desirable from the age of 15 onwards, and she knew it; revelling in the attentions of the local lads before she always broke their hearts. She knew that her destiny lay in society and after a trip to London – where she was particularly captivated by a trip to the theatre – her father knew that there would be no holding her.

Luckily, the escape route came in a fashion that even she thought would never happen. She snared the affections, in 1874, of

Edward Langtry, who was the witless heir to an Irish shipping fortune, when he docked his private yacht on the island in the search of hedonistic pleasure. It came his way in the shape of Lillie, who won him over with her beauty.

'To become the mistress of the yacht, I married the owner,' she would later say with wicked delight, and thus earned her passport, at the age of 21, out of Jersey. Soon she was the toast of London society, the must-have invitation for all the correct balls and dinner parties. The Countess of Warwick, who was also to enjoy Bertie's bed during his ladykilling period, remarked after meeting her at one such function: 'We were magnetised by her unique personality. How can words convey the vitality, the glow, the amazing charm that made this fascinating woman the centre of any group that she entered?'

Such vitality and glow would soon come to warm the cockles – and much else besides – of the heart of the Prince of Wales. Lillie had met the renowned portrait painter George Francis Miles at a London party. He asked her to pose for him. Soon the delicious portrait he painted was

Above: *Lillie Langtry, the actress who captured the heart of a future king.*

Left: *A stern-faced Edward VII and Alexandra at Sandringham in 1864.*

'TO BECOME THE MISTRESS OF THE YACHT, I MARRIED THE OWNER,' LILY SAID WITH WICKED DELIGHT

Above: *Sarah Bernhardt, another actress from the days of the Belle Epoque, who captured the heart of Bertie.*

WITHIN THREE WEEKS IT WAS PILLOW TALK AS THE FATHER-OF-SIX FELL HOPELESSLY IN LOVE WITH HER

built her a house in Bournemouth which was used for country trysts, hired an apartment in Paris for continental trysts and used the lodgings of a friend in London for capital trysts. Abroad, in places like the famous Maxim's restaurant in Paris, he brazenly flirted with Lillie, once even going as far as a full-mouthed kiss in front of all the other diners. Such actions could not escape the attentions of the newspaper writers abroad, but in Britain the press played a game of self-censorship which effectively gave sanction to his cavortings.

Such infidelity on a grand scale was more than the wretched Edward Langtry could bear. After he learned that Bertie had brazenly introduced his mistress to the Queen and Princess Alexandra he plunged into a vortex of alcohol abuse from which there was neither redemption nor escape. He died penniless, cadging drinks from anyone who wanted to hear the stories of how he had lost his beautiful wife to the next King of England.

THE COMMON TOUCH

Like the modern-day Princess of Wales, the Jersey Lillie was becoming very popular with the ordinary people. She was cheered and waved at in public, and her dresses were instantly copied. If she wore a dress to Ascot or Sadler's Wells one week, it was guaranteed to have been copied for the fancy West End stores by the following week. Edward had achieved one small victory over hypocrisy in that he flaunted his mistress. But the power of Victorian morality repressed any public 'crowing' over such a dubious triumph and his wish for her to be fully recognised by the royal family as his 'official' mistress for all public functions was never granted.

It was only natural for a man like Bertie that his roving eye would take him elsewhere. He passed on Lillie to Prince Louis of Battenberg, father to Earl Mountbatten, while he took his pleasure with the French actress Sarah Bernhardt. The affair with Lillie had lasted almost four years and there was no acrimony on either side when it ended in 1880 when she became pregnant and was forced to go to France to have his illegitimate child in secret. Upon her return she was no longer the society dame she had once been. Lillie yearned for the public

appearing on greetings cards which sold all over London. Prince Edward saw one of these cards and, by royal command, ordered it to be arranged that he too should get to meet the lovely lady about whom all London was talking.

In May 1877, a dinner party thrown by a bachelor friend of the Prince had Lillie Langtry – and her somewhat gormless husband – in attendance. From the moment he clapped eyes on her, Bertie schemed to have her. Lillie, too, was now skilled in the art of secret lovemaking, having had several 'menfriends' since persuading her husband to bring her to London. At the dinner party it was small talk between Bertie and Lillie. Within three weeks it was pillow talk as the father-of-six fell hopelessly in love with her.

Bertie seemed to go out of his way to flaunt his new mistress, forever testing the boundaries by which his life as prospective monarch of the realm was governed. He

limelight that she had once enjoyed so much and found it in the theatre.

She called upon Bertie to pull some strings with the West End crowd and was rewarded with a part in a play called *She Stoops To Conquer*. The Prince of Wales and many other distinguished members of society were there to cheer her on at opening night – even though reviewers in the newspapers were not so kind the following day. One said: 'As a novice, she should first learn the art of acting.' Lillie didn't care about the negative press and set about touring Britain with a repertory company she formed before sailing to America where she captivated the people. In 1892 she visited the town of Vinegaroon in Texas where Judge Roy Bean was so smitten by her he ended up changing the town's statute to permanently name it Langtry!

Lillie returned to Britain and married baronet Hugo de Bathe in 1897, moving with him to France where she spent the best part of the next two decades. She died in 1929 and was buried in St. Saviour's churchyard in Jersey, the island where she was born and from which she had longed only to escape. She had been to the funeral 19 years earlier of a man the public used to nickname Edward the Caresser. History knows him better as King Edward.

Above: *Lillie Langtry, the 'Jersey Lily', who inveigled her way into London society.*

Left: *The boudoir where Lillie's trysts with Edward took place.*

THE PUBLIC USED TO NICKNAME HIM EDWARD THE CARESSER. HISTORY KNOWS HIM BETTER AS KING EDWARD

EDWARD AND MRS SIMPSON

While King Edward VII's fling with Lillie Langtry could be dismissed by some as mere philanderings which placed no strain upon the fabric of monarchy or British life, the future King Edward VIII's swooning love affair with an American divorcee called Wallis Simpson did exactly the opposite. His infatuation with this woman would not only cost him his crown – it would drive the nation to the brink of its gravest constitutional crisis in centuries.

At a time when the empire and the commonwealth were needed most at the side of the Mother Country – when the storm clouds of war were gathering over Europe – this ineffectual, weak man's love was stronger for him, and more necessary to him, than any instinct to obey his call of duty. Edward was a weak man governed by a strong woman – a woman who, in the end, did not get her wish to be Queen.

ABANDONING THE THRONE

Before it broke upon the British public and the world in a storm-tide of publicity, Edward had been nurturing the secret of his plans for months. In his heart he had already chosen to abandon his throne for the woman he loved – now it was a matter of choosing the right moment to do it and under what circumstances. A court Press far more restrained than the tabloid gossip-mongers of today, and a code of silence among the echelons of the aristocracy, worked in his favour to keep the affair silent. But it could not last forever.

Edward VIII was King of England for 326 days before he abdicated for the woman he loved. The love affair had gone on for three years – an amazing length of time to keep a secret from a world that devoured news about the greatest surviving monarchy with alacrity. He had met Wallis Simpson in 1931, a 34-year-old American divorcee who people regarded as witty, if a little plain, and charming, but endowed with a tart tongue when she chose to use it.

She had had an upbringing as far removed from the House of Windsor as it would be possible to get; her father was a businessman from Maryland who had died when she was five and she had been raised in Baltimore by her mother. As a young

> EDWARD VIII WAS KING OF ENGLAND FOR 326 DAYS BEFORE HE ABDICATED FOR THE WOMAN HE LOVED

Above: *The Duke and Duchess of Windsor. She could never be queen, so he gave up his throne.*

lady she was always stricken by the sight of men in uniform – and in 1916 married a naval pilot, admitting to friends that she found the sight of his dress uniform and medals 'irresistible!' She was also drawn to a particular kind of lifestyle – one of parties, champagne, ballgowns and dances – like a moth to a flame, even though she had experienced none of it while growing up. She was, in fact, a social climber of the highest order.

Her marriage to Earl Winfield Spencer was short lived. The salary of a naval pilot was hardly enough to keep her in the manner to which she wanted to become accustomed and they parted in 1922. Her second marriage followed in 1928 to an Anglo-American businessman named Ernest Simpson who headed the London office of his wealthy family's shipping company.

For Wallis, the combination was thrilling – wealth and London, the society capital, rolled into one.

In 1929, she arrived to settle in the capital permanently, leaving behind forever the low social order of her formative years. In London she became something of a hit on the social circuit, recognised as a competent and amusing hostess who was never anything but charming to her guests.

She moved among lords and ladies, marquesses and duchesses – and she did it with a style which suggested she was a natural! But while she soared up the social barometer, her own marriage to the staid workaholic Ernest was headed for poor weather. Rows over his dullness and her champagne-soaked extravagances drove a wedge between them.

In December 1930, a dinner party that was to have extraordinary consequences for all concerned was hosted by Wallis Simpson at her splendid London home. The guests were Benjamin Thaw, new first secretary of the American embassy in London, his wife Consuelo and her sister Thelma, Viscountess of Furness. Lady Furness was described as a vampish figure who fancied herself as a cross between a Hollywood actress and a music hall queen, a woman of ravishing beauty and a stunning secret. For she was the current mistress of the Prince of Wales, the future King of England. Eventually a friendship blossomed between the three women and Wallis was soon privy to the secret affair being conducted by Thelma.

THE PRIZE CATCH

Eventually the Simpsons dined with the Prince and Wallis was spellbound. Because she knew of his intimacies, his likes and dislikes, his manner and his substance, she was able to perform as the most perfect guest. But in her heart she had started scheming to take this prize catch away from Thelma. Landing the Prince would take her out of the mainstream of high society into the stratosphere – and that is exactly what she planned to do.

Soon she and her husband were regular visitors to his country retreat and he reciprocated, increasingly without Thelma, at the Simpsons' flat off of Oxford Street in London. In January 1934, with Thelma still

unaware of the predatory ambitions of her new 'friend' she said to Wallis: 'I am off to the United States on a trip. Please will you look after the Prince to make sure he isn't lonely?' She looked after him all right – so much so that by the time Thelma returned in the spring, they were lovers.

Edward was a weak man, someone who looked for a maternal, strong streak in a woman – and he found it with Wallis Simpson. She doted on him because he was the entree to a world she had only ever dreamed about. But he genuinely needed her, needed her love and attention and strength the way a child needs its mother. It would forever remain a lopsided relationship, never a true partnership in the sense that most healthy relationships should be.

> WALLIS SIMPSON DOTED ON EDWARD BECAUSE HE WAS THE ENTREE TO A WORLD SHE HAD ONLY EVER DREAMED ABOUT

Below: *Edward's marriage to Simpson, a divorced American, shook the British establishment to the core.*

It was nothing new – indeed, seen as nothing wrong – for a member of the royal family like Edward to have affairs. It was the maintenance of secrecy which was all important. A small clique of his friends rapidly knew about the affair, even though they found the chemistry between the two strange to say the least. Love letters released many years later, after Wallis's death at the age of 89 in 1986, showed that he was infantile and pleading in his need for love and affection.

She was stern, admonishing, sensible. This showed through in their day-to-day attitudes towards each other. He was completely and utterly captivated by her. His friends said they could never recall a time when he looked so happy or so sad in equal amounts. A look from her could trigger euphoria like a drug or plunge him into the darkest moods. Slender, sophisticated and witty, as opposed to his shy, awkward, fumbling demeanour, it seemed as if she was the one who had been born into this lineage, not him.

DANGEROUS LIAISONS

Soon the discretion which was supposed to govern such dangerous liaisons of the heart was shed as the Prince, like a proud schoolboy showing off his latest toy, took her around the watering holes of Europe on whirlwind tours. Paris, Rome, Budapest, Monte Carlo – soon even the British Press was having to take note as their foreign rivals filled columns of newsprint every day with their glorious partying.

But the implacable British press barons like Rothermere and Beaverbrook, men committed to the notion of a solid and trustworthy establishment, kept the shenanigans from the readers of their newspapers, believing that trivia would only damage the crown and ultimately the country. Better, they believed, that the man in the street did not know of the strange frenzy of love that was gripping the future king. In America, there was no such hesitation among the Republicans. 'Queen Wally' screamed one newspaper headline as it delved into lurid details about the sleeping arrangements between them during one tour in Yugoslavia and Greece.

In January 1936, Edward became king, taking on all the rights and responsibilities

which the highest office demanded of him. His affair was known in the highest reaches of society – but it remained just that; a dalliance, a whim, an amusing diversion. No-one suspected that Edward would suggest anything as absurd as marriage to Wallis – something that would never have been sanctioned because, as head of the Church of England, he was forbidden to marry a divorced woman.

ROCKING THE ESTABLISHMENT

Some weeks before the death of his father, which placed him upon the throne, Edward had spoken with Prime Minister Stanley Baldwin, informing him of Wallis's intention to proceed with divorce from her husband. Baldwin was horrified. He knew that the Press turned a blind eye to his dalliance with a married woman – but a divorced one! The shock for the establishment would be too much to bear. He begged Edward to get Wallis to reconsider a divorce, but Edward told him: 'It would be wrong for me to attempt to influence Mrs. Simpson just because she happens to be a friend of the King. I have no right to interfere with the affairs of an individual.' Baldwin, for his part, was amazed at the self-delusion that Edward seemed to be stricken with. It was as if he fully expected to be allowed to 'carry on' with her as always and expect people to ignore it. But the conspiracy of silence ended months after his accession to the throne. There was an eight-day period after it when Edward wavered between duty and love – and history records which won in the end.

The silence ended when the Bishop of Bradford, Dr. Blunt, chastised him for his 'carefree' lifestyle which was out of keeping with the economically-hard times and the teachings of the church, which he represented. The newspapers could no longer ignore it. The British establishment, so pliable at times in turning away its face in matters of discretion, now met the crisis full on and the matter was splashed over the newspapers. Edward had fully expected the British people and the establishment to come over to his side in the matter. He wanted to marry Wallis and place her upon the throne next to him. The very suggestion

Above: *The newspapers at first held off the crisis, then enjoyed a field day.*

Opposite Top: *Wallis Simpson, found by the noble family of the realm to be altogether unsuitable to wear the crown of queen.*

Opposite Bottom: *Stanley Baldwin, whose government kept the lid on the crisis until it could no longer be contained.*

EDWARD WANTED TO MARRY WALLIS AND PLACE HER UPON THE THRONE NEXT TO HIM

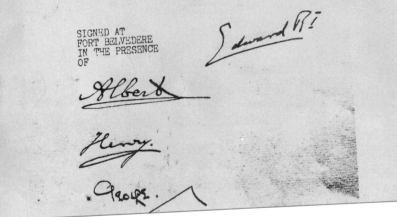

INSTRUMENT OF ABDICATION

I, Edward the Eighth, of Great Britain, Ireland, and the British Dominions beyond the Seas, King, Emperor of India, do hereby declare My irrevocable determination to renounce the Throne for Myself and for My descendants, and My desire that effect should be given to this Instrument of Abdication immediately.

In token whereof I have hereunto set My hand this tenth day of December, nineteen hundred and thirty six, in the presence of the witnesses whose signatures are subscribed.

SIGNED AT
FORT BELVEDERE
IN THE PRESENCE
OF

Edward RI

Albert

Henry

George

Above: *The abdication letter in which Edward VIII relinquished the crown over Wallis Simpson.*

Right: *Edward caused a great deal of controversy when he met Adolf Hitler in 1937.*

THE MONARCH, LIKE KING CHARLES AGAINST CROMWELL, WAS ON THE LOSING SIDE

threw his mother Queen Mary into apoplexy. There was an emergency council of war at Buckingham Palace which was attended also by Baldwin.

When he announced to Baldwin his intention to marry, the PM replied: 'We will not have it, sir. People are talking about you and this American woman. I have had so many nasty letters from people who respected your father and who do not appreciate the way you are going on.' Edward, baffled, became convinced that there was some kind of conspiracy aimed directly at him. All he could mumble was 'poor, poor Wallis'.

She, meanwhile, became the target of a fearful campaign of hate in which bricks and stones were hurled through the windows of her London residence and children sang outside the door: 'Hark the Herald Angels sing, Mrs. Simpson's Pinched our King!' She packed her bags the first night of the 'crisis' and fled to the South of France on the first night train. Edward stayed behind to wrestle with the establishment and his own conscience. He set about trying to lobby the high and mighty, who might sway opinion in his favour.

THE GREAT DEBATE

One curious ally was staunch monarchist Winston Churchill – perhaps because his mother was American too. One anecdote recalls a lunch he enjoyed with playwright Noel Coward in which Churchill said: 'Why shouldn't he marry his cutie?' To which Coward replied: 'Because England doesn't want a Queen Cutie!'

An idea proposed by Esmond Harmsworth, of the *Daily Mail* publishing empire, seemed to offer the best solution of all. Esmond said that he might try wooing his mother with the idea of a morganatic marriage, the compromise whereby she would be his wife but would have no claim to any titles within the British royal family, and neither would her children. The Queen would not accept it. The cabinet would not accept it. It had become a battle of wills between constitutional rulers and the constitutional monarch. The monarch, like King Charles against Cromwell, was to end up on the losing side.

The King was hopelessly and irreversibly in love with Wallis Simpson. Duty

became an alien word to him. Everything he was brought up for, nurtured for, was scattered and destroyed by that strongest of emotions. In the end, after having discussed it with Wallis, he decided to abdicate, to forfeit his inalienable right to rule for the woman he could not rule without. Later, in her memoirs, Wallis wrote of how she wept when she heard the abdication speech on the wireless on 11 December 1936. She said: 'I was lying on the sofa with my hands over my eyes, trying to hide my tears'. The King had told the nation and the empire that he could not rule alone.

He left for France and did not return to live in Britain again. Wallis and Edward, now given the courtesy titles of Duke and Duchess of Windsor, caused a furore in 1937 when they were seen as guests of Hitler, but they did not disgrace their country by choosing to live in Germany during the war. Edward became governor of the

*Above: **The happy couple on their wedding day in France.***

WALLIS AND EDWARD CAUSED A FURORE IN 1937 WHEN THEY WERE GUESTS OF HITLER

Bahamas during the war years and the couple settled afterwards in Paris in a splendid white chateau for which they paid a peppercorn rent. They married in a simple ceremony in the Loire Valley and remained as exiles from the House of Windsor for the rest of their days. He died in 1972 at the age of 77; she died 14 years later.

There was a certain bitter irony at Edward's funeral, which was held at St. George's Chapel, Windsor. Wallis was there for the occasion, confronting the heirs to this contradictory, somewhat cold, often hypocritical family. She was allowed to stay one night at Buckingham Palace before journeying back to Paris and obscurity. On her dressing room table she kept a message written by Edward which read: 'My friend, with thee, to live alone, methinks were better than to own a crown, a sceptre and a throne.' Truly, if nothing much else was worthy in his character, Edward did possess and nourish a love that was Olympian in its magnitude.

PRINCESS MARGARET

Affairs of the heart have plagued the House of Windsor in the same way some families inherit genetic disorders. But perhaps none was sadder, or more poignant, than that between Group Captain Peter Townsend and Princess Margaret, the relationship which started as a schoolgirl infatuation and went on to develop into a deep and abiding love. Ironically, Princess Margaret won the kind of backing and public support for her forbidden romance which was denied to King Edward VIII – but it still did her no good. In the 1950s, Britain was still a place where the order of things was dictated by tradition and conformity. Even though the swinging sixties, free love and sex before marriage was just around the corner, for Princess Margaret they might as well have been on the moon.

Margaret was a beautiful 14-year-old schoolgirl when she first met the dashing flier Townsend. The 29-year-old war hero, his uniform bemedalled for valour in the Battle of Britain and other airborne conflicts, was assigned to Buckingham Palace as an equerry to King George VI. Townsend was the epitome of a young girl's romantic ideal. He was tall, good looking, charming, brave and sensitive.

To a young woman aware of her own sexuality just beginning to blossom, he was an idol and she worshipped him as such. It was 1944 and the war was not yet won, but the royal family had garnered massive public affection during the worst of the blitz for refusing to leave London. Princess Margaret was turning into the most beautiful of the King's daughters and her adolescent life fascinated the royal watchers of the Press. Soon she would really give them something to write about.

Townsend was given a house in the grounds of Windsor Castle where he lived with his pretty wife Rosemary. Margaret sought him out as often as she could, asking him advice on any subject under the sun. Of course, it was all done merely so she could get breathlessly close to the man she was beginning to hero-worship.

A LONG SEPARATION

In 1947, at 17, she set sail with her sister, Princess Elizabeth, later to become queen of a tormented household, on a tour of South Africa. The tour, a three-month long marathon, was planned as a test of the love that Prince Philip of Greece proferred for Princess Elizabeth. He had been courting her for some time and the King felt that a long separation would test the feelings of both of them. But where Elizabeth felt only sadness at such an enforced separation, there was joy in Margaret's heart because Group Captain Townsend was accompanying them. And Rosemary was staying at home. Later a royal aide would recall: 'A smile of pure joy crossed Margaret's face when she heard that Captain Townsend was to join the party. She could not believe her luck.'

On the ships, on the verandahs of the African hotels, with the southern stars twinkling above them, Margaret drifted off into a romantic dream world as she stayed up late listening to the wit and wisdom of the cultured Townsend. A shiver began running through royal ranks that there was a replay of the abdication crisis of 1936 fomenting itself, but the King, who was close to both his daughters, believed that it was nothing more than a girlish infatuation for a handsome, decorated warrior.

But Margaret was obviously scheming for something much, much more than passing affection from her hero airman. In

Above: *Princess Margaret, a royal beauty without peer. But her love for Group Captain Townsend (right) led to a disastrous romance.*

Opposite Top: *Princess Margaret with the Governor of Mauritius, Sir Robert Scott, on the African tour where her love for Townsend grew stronger every day.*

Opposite Bottom: *A beaming Princess Elizabeth with Prince Philip of Greece, the man who became her fiancé. The course of true love was not so easy for Margaret.*

sive 'establishment' would doom them as it had doomed others before.

Once they were caught in an act of frolicking in Buckingham Palace itself. Townsend was carrying Margaret up a staircase, like a groom crossing the threshold of a honeymoon hotel with his new bride, when the King happened to come across them. He was flabbergasted at such intimacy, even though Margaret blurted out: 'I told him to do it papa, I ordered him!' Another time they were caught kissing by a footman in a drawing room and on another occasion were seen embracing by staff in a stairwell. Soon the affair was the talk of the palace.

Townsend had risen to the rank of Deputy Master of the Royal Household and knew that he was probably on borrowed time. But he used his position to arrange cosy weekends at country houses where he would be present with the Princess and they never, ever, displayed affection in public.

Their trysts were arranged within the palace but they never left it together. They

1951, having spurned many society suitors who would have given their right arms to squire around the beautiful, eligible bachelor girl at town and country balls, she saw her chance to develop a relationship with Townsend. He parted with his wife when the strain of long separations due to royal duties became too much for her to bear. Rosemary vanished from the house she shared with Townsend in Windsor Castle's grounds to move in with a lover. Townsend, who was now becoming as close to the princess as she was to him, said: 'We were not right for each other. We married in wartime and now in peacetime the marriage is over.'

The duo were riding through the grounds of Balmoral, Queen Victoria's favourite Scottish retreat, and it was then that she told him of her love for him. He returned it back with all his heart – but, wiser and older than her, perhaps knew it was doomed from the start. She was intoxicated by the twin drugs of youth and love – he knew better and believed that the all-perva-

Above: *Group Captain
Townsend in Brussels,
where he was stationed as
air attache.*

THE ROYAL FAMILY KNEW
CONCLUSIVELY ABOUT THE
RELATIONSHIP BUT DID NOT
MOVE TO BREAK IT UP

THE ESTABLISHMENT
BELIEVED THAT MARGARET
AND TOWNSEND'S
RELATIONSHIP WAS
SCANDALOUS

drove away in plain cars – often alone, for this was in the days before global terrorism – and spent precious moments at locations which are secret to this day. But they were like a modern day Romeo and Juliet – unable to live without one another, yet becoming increasingly aware that their romance was doomed.

Soon the whisperings of 'cradle snatching' began to pervade society, then the palace. Prince Philip, curmudgeonly patriarch of the post-war reign of the House of Windsor, was one of the biggest objectors. He regarded Townsend as nothing more than an 'employee' of the family firm and implored Elizabeth to work against the relationship. Margaret, who has a streak of determination running through her that is every bit as fierce as that belonging to her future brother-in-law, was determined to bring her affair out into the open – and get the 'establishment' to support her. It was not to work out.

She met with Sir Alan Lascelles, the Queen's private secretary, to enquire whether a divorce on Townsend's part, for admitted adultery by his wife, would stand in the way of their future happiness. Lascelles said, wrongly, that he could see no problem as long as a suitable period of time elapsed between the decree absolute and the publication of their burgeoning relationship. The royal family now knew conclusively about the relationship but did

not yet move to break it up. It was, after all, still contained within the walls of the palaces and houses of the Windsor tribe. But that all changed at a certain ceremony at Westminster Abbey.

It was the Coronation of Queen Elizabeth, her sister, in 1953, the most glorious of royal spectacles and the first one ever to be filmed by television cameras for those at home and those abroad in the remains of the empire and commonwealth. A keen-eyed Fleet Street reporter happened to glance at Princess Margaret leaning forward to brush off a speck of dust from the uniform of Group Captain Townsend as her sister moved regally up the aisle.

It was interpreted – correctly – as an act of love by a woman for her man and the information travelled around the world. Captain Townsend doubly confirmed the reporter's suspicion when he looked longingly into her eyes. Society columnists pulled in favours from aristocratic tipsters and informants and, sure enough, the story of the forbidden affair was given as much play the next day as the Coronation itself.

Even though Britain was slowly becoming a more liberal society, with more rights for women and class barriers being torn down, there was no such moral relaxation for the watchdogs of the establishment. They believed that Margaret and Townsend's relationship was scandalous, akin to the constitutional crisis of 17 years

Left: *Queen Elizabeth II at her coronation in Westminster Abbey. Margaret's act of brushing a piece of fluff from the suit of Group Captain Townsend during the ceremony set tongues wagging.*

earlier. It was nonsense, of course, especially as the divorce rate in Britain was soaring that year.

Margaret and Townsend's love affair could hardly be held up as tearing apart the moral fibre of the nation. But Churchill – the man who had held such kind words and thoughts for the lovestruck Edward all those years before – felt duty-bound to put the age-old honour of the monarchy before individual rights and dreams. He packed Margaret off on a tour of Rhodesia with her mother while Group Captain Townsend was exiled to the British Embassy in Brussels as air attache.

The affair continued, however, despite the obstacles placed in their way. It was conducted in secret love letters, in expensive international telephone calls and at out-of-the-way hotels and homes of friends. But just before Princess Margaret's 25th birthday her sister Elizabeth, as Queen and Head of the Church of England, told her that Winston Churchill had communicated the feelings of the cabinet to her. Those feelings were that Parliament would never, under any circumstances, sanction a marriage between her and Townsend. She

was faced with either dumping Townsend, or going off into social Siberia with him, exiled like the Duke of Windsor had been so many years before.

In October 1955 it came to an end. There was an enormous amount of public sympathy for her, but it was not enough to break the back of the establishment's power. Crowds had begun gathering outside

Below: *The end of the romance nears as Group Captain Townsend is quizzed by a reporter in Belgium about the affair.*

MARGARET WAS NOT AS FOPPISH, OR AS WEAK, AS THE FORMER KING EDWARD. SHE ULTIMATELY KNEW THAT HER DUTY LAY WITH THE MONARCHY

Clarence House, her London residence, screaming: 'Marry him! Marry him!' Editorials in some down-market newspapers begged for her to go her own way. But the pull of duty was ultimately stronger. She was not as foppish, or as weak, as the former King Edward. Margaret ultimately knew that her duty lay with the monarchy.

On Monday 31 October, she issued this statement: 'I would like it to be known that I have decided not to marry Group Captain Peter Townsend. I have been aware that subject to renouncing my rights of succession it might have been possible for me to contract a civil marriage. But mindful of the church's teaching that a Christian marriage is indissoluble, and conscious of my duty to the Commonwealth, I have resolved to put these considerations before any others.

'I have reached the decision entirely alone, and in doing so I have been strengthened by the unfailing support and devotion of Group Captain Townsend.' She went on to marry Lord Snowdon, a marriage which floundered in 1978 and finally ended in divorce. No man, say those who really know Margaret, ever lived up to her dashing war hero.

ANDREW AND FERGIE

The course of true love has never run smooth for Prince Andrew, the 'playboy prince' who of all the Queen's sons became the most dashing, daring and handsome. Unlike Edward, who cares not at all for the action-man life, and Prince Charles, who is keen on subjects like architecture and the environment, Prince Andrew revelled in the hurly burly of military life and was never happier than flying his beloved helicopters, or carousing in the mess with his warrior chums. And when it came to the 'fillies' as he was fond of calling them, none was more contentious, or would cause a bigger stir, than one soft-porn actress named Koo Stark.

Kathryn 'Koo' Stark was a gorgeous young woman of wealthy parents and a budding future as a film actress or photographer – she seemed to show promise in both fields. But she had erred, just once, in her judgement while trying to make her way to the top. She had made a movie called *Emily*, a soft-focus romp with well-endowed men and women getting into more positions than a Rubik's Cube. And that was why she could never, ever, be acceptable to the House of Windsor.

A DOOMED AFFAIR

British gossip writer Nigel Dempster claims that the duo were introduced at his home in London in 1982 during a party and that they corresponded with each other during the Falklands War. It was said from the early days that she possessed the wit, sophistication and sensitivity which he seemed to lack. Anyway, the chemistry between them was definitely there – even though the affair was doomed to die.

But not at first. Koo was a hit with the Queen and Queen Mother when introduced to them at Balmoral while the Duke of

Below: Prince Andrew, another royal who chose an unsuitable companion – Koo Stark.

Above: *Koo Stark in the soft-porn film* **Emily** *for which she was ever damned in the eyes of the royal family.*

Edinburgh – always one with a keen eye for the ladies – was entranced by her. It was only when the details of her foray into soft-porn began to seep out little by little that the pressure was increased on Andrew to end the affair.

Andrew was besotted with Koo, of that there can be no doubt. They wrote passionate love letters to each other, and they planned a future together. But that big D word among the Windsors – Duty – reared its head and, under direct orders from the Queen herself, Andrew was told to end the relationship forthwith in 1983. He did so, in a particularly cool and calculating manner.

Nigel Blundell and Sue Blackhall, in their authoritative work *The Fall of the House of Windsor* wrote: 'Their intense 18 month relationship ended in 1983 when the Queen and the Duke of Edinburgh became alarmed at the continuing furore over her soft-porn cinematic credits. Loyal at least to his mother, Andrew cut the poor girl dead. Without having the decency even to telephone her, he ordered the Buckingham Palace switchboard not to put her calls through to him.

'It was a callous, though perhaps royally predictable way of ending what had been an amazingly passionate love affair with a hugely loving and supporting young lady.'

But if the Queen and Prince Philip had known of the titanic convulsions within the royal family that one Sarah Ferguson would ultimately cause, then Koo Stark might well have seemed an almost ideal partner for their son.

It is generally believed that Andrew and Sarah Ferguson, his future wife and Duchess of York, who had known each other from their earliest childhood days because of Sarah's father Major Ron Ferguson's managership of Prince Charles' polo team, married on the rebound of true love – he for Koo Stark, she for a former racing driver and society dandy called Paddy McNally. After engineering an invitation to the palace in 1985 – aided and abetted by Princess Diana, her friend – the spark between Andrew and the red-haired

'IT WAS A CALLOUS, THOUGH PERHAPS ROYALLY PREDICTABLE WAY OF ENDING WHAT HAD BEEN AN AMAZINGLY PASSIONATE LOVE AFFAIR'

Above and Below: *The Duchess of York was taken to heart by the British public in the days before her marriage. But her PR image soon began to spin badly out of control.*

senting her as he did so with a splendid oval ruby surrounded by ten diamonds. Soon the nation was gushing over a new royal love match as the potteries began to turn out commemorative plates and jugs and other assorted paraphernalia.

A REGAL SPECTACLE

On 23 July the same year he led her up the aisle of Westminster Abbey as 500 million TV viewers around the world witnessed the spectacle which some say only the British can pull off with such majesty and panache. There was a lingering kiss on the balcony at Buckingham Palace, an open horse-drawn carriage ride through London and a helicopter to the royal yacht Britannia for a honeymoon in the Azores. This, thought the British public, was a match made in heaven. Never did two more vivacious, headstrong yet likeable people pledge their troth to join the ranks of the Windsor dynasty. Yet it was all going wrong before it started. Physically they had it all – their displays of affection for the press on public engagements and at photo-

beauty known as 'Fergie' to all her friends seemed to glow and intensify.

Their courtship was carried out at the country homes of discreet friends, places where details would never be whispered to the scoundrels in the tabloid press. At one such place, Floors Castle in Scotland, Andrew dropped to one knee on 19 March 1986 and proudly proposed to Sarah, pre-

Left: *The royal couple were unable to escape the cameras on their honeymoon.*

Below: *A visit to the races. But Andrew's shipboard service meant that Fergie was soon looking for solace.*

calls while on holiday were causing eyebrows to be raised in the Palace. They seemed literally incapable of keeping their hands off each other. But physical love is never enough in a relationship, let alone a marriage. In short, they had little to talk about once the lovemaking was over. He was still a sailor in love with the sea; she was intent on rising through the highest ranks of society. Somewhere down the road it seemed inevitable that their interests would not converge.

Fergie tried to play the dutiful wife, first by learning to become a helicopter pilot, which she believed would give her 'something to talk with him about when he comes home in the evening'. Unfortunately for her, he wasn't coming home all that often. Andrew truly loved the service life and in 1987 he went back to sea on the destroyer HMS Edinburgh. It was the long separations which would drive the wedge between them – and lead Fergie on her global gallivanting which would earn her the cruel nickname 'Freebie Fergie' from

Above: *Major Ron Ferguson with Sarah. He had his own secrets, such as visiting a London massage parlour for extra services of a sexual nature.*

THE PICTURES WERE PROOF THAT PHILANDERING WAS ALL PART OF THE GAME WITHIN THE MONARCHY

---

the press as she swanned from one exotic location to another, seemingly without a care in the world.

In May 1988 Major Ron Ferguson was caught in a classic Sunday newspaper expose as being the frequenter of a London massage parlour which offered considerably more to its clientele than a back rub. The royal family rallied around Major Ron, although Andrew was furious, seeing the incident as a major slur upon his choice of partner in marriage.

The birth of Princess Beatrice, their first daughter, seemed to gloss over the scandal and actually served to bring them closer together for a while. There was more hap-

piness too in March 1990 when Princess Eugenie, their second, was born. But Andrew was only able to snatch brief weekends with his family as he was at sea most of the time. The cracks began to show as Fergie became the most knocked royal in living memory in the newspapers. She was Frumpy Fergie when an outfit was deemed inappropriate. She was Fat Fergie when compared with gorgeous Diana, and Freeloading Fergie when off on another jaunt to somewhere exotic. And she was reeling under the strain of a marriage that allowed her and Andrew just 42 days together during the whole of that year.

Insiders to the clan say that he was immersing himself more and more in shipboard life, always feeling let down by the humdrum existence of a day-to-day life on dry land. The ghastly modern mansion they had built at Sunninghill in Berkshire – nicknamed Southyork or the Dallas Palace because of its gauche style – was the scene of many parties, but none of them attended by him. He seemed happy to slump in front of a TV set and watch old war videos whenever he was home. Fergie was beginning to look elsewhere for companionship – and perhaps even love.

NEW ROMANCE

In that same year Fergie went to North Africa with a rich Texan called Steve Wyatt, heir to a Houston oil fortune, and, later, on his private jet to the South of France. In 1992, this holiday came to haunt her when 120 photos of the two together – including one of Wyatt with his arm around Princess Beatrice – were mysteriously found in a London flat and printed in a daily newspaper. For Andrew it was the last straw. He told the Queen in a private audience that he could stand many things, but being a cuckolded husband wasn't one of them. He wanted out of the marriage, saying he realised now that it had been a mistake from the word go.

The Queen sympathised and realised herself just what a disaster the pictures were; it was the proof (which the royals had hidden so successfully for so many years) that philandering was all part of the game within the monarchy. The Queen, however, did her best to try to keep the marriage together – without success.

Both sides called in lawyers and on 19 March a terse statement was issued from Buckingham Palace to the effect that the couple was separating. It made no mention of a divorce – Princess Anne would later be the first offspring of Her Majesty to inflict that upon the royal household.

'In view of the media speculation which the Queen finds especially undesirable during the general election campaign,' the statement said, 'Her Majesty is issuing the following statement. Last week lawyers acting for the Duchess of York initiated discussions about a formal separation for the Duke and Duchess. These discussions are not yet completed and nothing will be said until they are. The Queen hopes that the media will spare the Duke and Duchess of York and their children any intrusion.'

This was a crisis unparalleled within the royal family for years and Fleet Street pursued the story with a vengeance. Soon it transpired that there had been some sort of dirty-tricks campaign against Fergie within the walls of Buckingham Palace itself, with advisers to the Queen laying down misinformation about the Duchess. Despite huffy denials to the contrary at first, Her

Majesty's press secretary Charles Anson was later to issue a humble apology to the Duchess in which he admitted making unauthorised remarks after a press briefing.

But there was worse – much worse – for the royal family and the British public to come. In 1992 Fergie took up with a dashing, balding man named Johnny Bryan,

Above: *Fergie cuddles her children Beatrice and Eugenie on a Swiss slope.*

Top: *Happy families – the Duke, Duchess, Beatrice, Eugenie and grandfather Major Ron.*

described as a 'financial adviser'. It did not take the wolverine British press long to dig up the facts on Mr. Bryan – and discover that he was a close friend of, and social gadfly with, one Steve Wyatt, the Texan who had caused such distress to the royal household in the first place. There was an exotic holiday in Thailand and Indonesia while Prince Andrew stuck his square jaw out at home and tried to put a brave face on an increasingly distressing situation.

A CLOSE ADVISER

Royal gossips said that Bryan was indeed advising Fergie on financial matters; mainly on the settlement that she should receive when she pushed the ultimate panic button in Buckingham Palace and pressed for a divorce. But there was surely something unique about his style of 'advising' when the next shock was to hit the establishment like a speeding rocket.

In August 1992, they went away together again, with the children, to a villa in the south of France. A cunning French paparazzi photographer had crawled in the undergrowth, unbeknown to them, to capture on colour film just what a unique advising style it was! There were topless pictures of Fergie. There was Bryan sucking her big toe. There was Bryan massaging suntan oil on her and gently tucking her hair behind the back of her neck. And all of it was done in front of her two children and two male bodyguards. A unique style of money management indeed!

The photographs earned photographer Daniel Angelli a fortune from British tabloids and European magazines, reducing Fergie's already low status to zero. Andrew was humiliated beyond belief, with one newspaper, the *Daily Star*, saying in a leader column: 'This silly strumpet has behaved in a way which would disgrace a council house, let alone a palace.'

In a symbolic gesture, Fergie left Balmoral the morning the pictures were published in her car, a modern day banishment after the photos of her dreadful performance were served up at the royal breakfast table along with the kippers and the kedgeree.

A few months later there was more misery in the House of Ferguson when Major Ron was exposed again by a 26-year-old former stablegirl called Lesley Player who wrote a book about her affair with Major Ron and other assorted royal romps, including Fergie's fling with Steve Wyatt – someone, she claimed, who also bedded her. It was all too much to bear for the embattled royal family.

PRINCESS ANNE

The first divorce, however, came from an unexpected quarter. Princess Anne, who started off as the most unloved royal in the eyes of the public, ended up carving herself out a unique position of affection thanks to her tireless work on behalf of charities, such as Save the Children. Born in August 1950, she grew up with all the privileges of

Below: *Ron Ferguson and Lesley Player – another kiss-and-tell beauty who heaped more embarrassment on the House of Windsor.*

the inglorious moment for newspaper history. Another time a newspaper man mistakenly called her 'love' while attempting to take her picture and she erupted in fury at him. She was, therefore, hardly the darling of the brood.

She had been married, almost a decade earlier, in 1973, to Captain Mark Phillips. Phillips, a dour, humourless sort, was an army officer known as 'Foggie' to

the royal household and seemed to be developing into an acerbic-tongued hothead by the time she was a teenager. Like her father the Duke, from whom she seems to have inherited her temper and her inability to suffer fools gladly, Princess Anne hated the royal press corps which followed her every move – and let them know it.

In 1982, when she fell off her horse at the Badminton Horse Trials, she screamed 'naff off' to cameramen seeking to record

Above: *Princess Anne and Captain Mark Phillips in 1981, before the irreparable rift that grew between them.*

Above Right: *Princess Anne found solace in her work with children around the world.*

his mess room chums because he was 'thick and wet'. A man from the shires with a love of the countryside, shooting, riding and assorted other pursuits of the tweedy set, Mark seemed a splendid match for Anne, who had had a succession of boyfriends without ever seeming to be serious about any of them.

The couple married on 14 November 1973 at Westminster Abbey with all the pomp and circumstance of state surround-

Above: *The Queen and Princess Anne with royal children Peter and Zara. Of all the Queen's children, Anne is said to be closest to her.*

ing them. It seemed a match made in heaven – and even if Anne was a bit sour-faced sometimes, seemingly pompous and rude on others, the ecstatic thousands who turned out to wish them well on the wedding day seemed to indicate that even the frostiest of the royals was deserving of the fidelity of the masses.

After a couple of years the Queen parted with some of her immense wealth and bought them the £5,000,000 mansion Gatcombe Park in Gloucestershire where royal offspring Peter and Zara would spend their formative years. If people were expecting the Princess Royal to spend her life shooting pheasants and riding in the local hunt they were disappointed. If anything, domestic life disagreed immensely with her.

She found herself bored by the constraints of staying at home and as she turned 30 plunged into work. Her list of public engagements grew, her travels to perilous, dirty places abroad enhanced her public image as a royal who really cared

> ANNE WAS A BIT SOUR-FACED SOMETIMES, AND SEEMED POMPOUS AND RUDE ON OTHER OCCASIONS

about the ordinary people of the world and her marriage to Mark Phillips seemed merely of secondary importance.

It was in 1984 that the first whispers of marital discord began circulating in places of power. Both were at the Los Angeles Olympics as part of the equestrian team – and they slept in separate accommodation. In society there were reports of bitchiness and pointed exchanges between them on the occasions when they were seen together at balls and dinner parties. But it was to be the extraordinary revelations of a former royal bodyguard which first gave the hint as to how deep the trouble might be between them.

DAMAGING RUMOURS

In 1985 Peter Cross, her former 'minder,' touted round Fleet Street tabloids – for an asking price said to be over £500,000 – the story that he and she had enjoyed a 'special relationship' together. So special, he alleged that she even telephoned him on the night baby Zara was born. He boasted that she was in love with him, but the palace weathered the scandal as Fleet Street exposed him as a man who had enjoyed several affairs during his marriage. Nevertheless, the 'no smoke without fire' school of commentators believed that the damage was done.

By the following year, the marriage was damaged beyond repair but Anne, who is imbued with as much sense of duty as her mother, insisted that they should stay together for the sake of the children and the nation. In 1986, a naval officer who would later steal her heart began working for the Queen as an equerry.

Tall and handsome, Timothy Laurence moved with grace and charm through the palace and court life, liked by everyone, including her Majesty, and her daughter, who was by this time thoroughly miserable with her own lot. A lack of spark on her husband's part, his worries about money and the gradual drift between them since the heady day that they had walked up the aisle at Westminster Abbey together had combined to destroy her love for him and place passions elsewhere.

THE NEW ATTRACTION

It wasn't until 1989 that the world learned of the attraction between Anne and Commander Laurence. A number of personal letters written by him to her – emotional love letters to be exact – had been stolen from her briefcase and posted to *The Sun* newspaper. For once that salacious organ did the decent thing and refused to publish any of their contents and the letters were returned intact to the Princess Royal. But they showed to the public that yet another crisis was about to break over the bows of the ship of state and in less than four months the terse statement came from Buckingham Palace that the couple were to separate, with no plans for divorce.

Anne and Mark remained friends, determined to be civilised about the whole thing. Their love of horses and other pursuits meant they still met at functions, and they never seemed to harbour any animosity towards each other. But in March 1991, there was yet more trouble in store for the royal family. A 40-year-old New Zealand art teacher named Heather Tonkin named Captain Phillips as the father of her six-year-old child, and launched a paternity suit against him.

Below and Bottom: *Anne with her new husband, Naval Commander Timothy Laurence.*

She said that she had conceived the child on a night of passion at a hotel in Auckland in November 1984 when she was 31 and Captain Phillips 35. She alleged that some £40,000 in maintenance money had been paid over the years – disguised as 'equestrian' fees – but that she was seeking more because of the reputed £1,000,000 he was supposed to be getting from the royal purse for parting with Anne. Eventually the paternity suit was dropped, probably because of an out-of-court settlement reached between the two parties.

On 13 April 1992, Princess Anne became the second royal since Margaret to get divorced. There was a statement from Buckingham Palace as the nation turned its eyes heavenwards, wondering what next to expect in the ongoing royal pantomime. Harold Brooks Baker, editor of *Debretts Peerage*, took the view that divorce among the royal family was no longer a tragedy, saying: 'Because the Princess Royal has served her country so well she will be the first royal to re-marry with her parents' approval. The public will also approve because they respect her so much.'

To save embarrassment for her mother, as head of the Church of England, Princess Anne chose that re-marriage to take place in the Church of Scotland. She married the commander on Saturday 13 December at the modest Crathie parish church near Balmoral, watched by about 30 family and friends. She had, it seems, proved Brooks Baker correct; of all the royals, next to Her Majesty and the Queen mum, she remains the most treasured.

PRINCESS MICHAEL OF KENT

So much for the wayward hormones, wretched marriages and shattered secrets in the House of Windsor. But it was an inherited blemish from the royal they all called

Above: *Princess Pushy, otherwise known as Princess Michael of Kent.*

> IN APRIL 1985 IT WAS REVEALED THAT PRINCESS MICHAEL OF KENT'S FATHER HAD BEEN A MEMBER OF HITLER'S DREADED SS

'Princess Pushy' which several years earlier had plunged the House of Windsor into crisis. In April 1985 it was revealed that Princess Michael of Kent's father had been a member of Hitler's dreaded SS!

Baron Gunther von Reibnitz, her aristocratic German father, had joined the ranks of Hitler's cruellest servants – the men who ran the death camps, who massacred innocent prisoners of war and civilians and against whom many thousands of Britons had died.

The Baron, Nazi party member 412855, was not involved in ghastly medical experiments, nor had he any part to play in the evil genocide of the Jews. But he joined the

Left: *The notorious SS, of which Princess Michael's father was a member.*

Below: *Simon Wiesenthal, Nazi hunter, ascertained that her father was involved in the awful SS baby farms.*

Nazi party as a volunteer and was closely involved in the SS 'Lebensborn' programme, the Nazi baby farms where Hitler urged strapping SS men to breed with Nordic maidens in pursuit of his twisted master race. Nazi war criminal hunter Simon Wiesenthal said from his office in Vienna: 'It is evident that he was an early enthusiast – someone who joined the party very early on in the 1920s.'

THE SS CONNECTION

The story broke in tabloid newspapers on the eve of its publication in detailed historical books. It hit hardest among veterans and monarchy fanatics – the idea that an SS man's daughter was in the upper echelons of the House of Windsor! There was a public outcry followed by frantic meetings at Buckingham Palace between the Queen and Princess Michael.

This time there would be no question of banishment or disgrace. The Queen, on the advice of her ministers, agreed that it was a distasteful episode and that no-one could deny the immediate impact it had had upon the royal household. But she confirmed that the sins of the father were not to be visited upon the daughter.

And the following day Princess Michael became more popular than she had in years when she went on TV to speak about the affair. She said: 'Here I am, 40 years old, and I suddenly discover something that is

really quite unpleasant. I shall just simply have to live with it. It was a very, very great blow because I have always hero-worshipped him.' Princess Michael went on to state that she had a document which proved that her father's membership of the Black Guard of Nazism was 'honorary'. She added: 'He never served with the SS, he never wore the uniform.'

Nazi hunter Wiesenthal, himself a death camp survivor who lost some 80 members of his family in the extermination centres, described her claim that he was an honorary member of the SS as 'nonsense'. But he did help to defuse the scandal for the Princess by saying: 'He did not work in a concentration camp. Had he done so I would have been aware of it. However, he added: 'He pledged his ideals to Hitler, and the Hitler ideals and hatreds, very early on.

Above: *Princess Diana, when she was Lady Diana Spencer and on the verge of becoming engaged to Prince Charles.*

Right: *The happy couple upon the announcement of their engagement.*

PRINCESS MICHAEL'S FATHER PLEDGED HIMSELF TO HITLER'S IDEALS AND HATREDS VERY EARLY ON

It doesn't make him whiter than white.' Princess Michael weathered the storm, but she would have to live with the stigma of it for the rest of her days.

CHARLES AND DIANA

No scandal, however, in recent or ancient times, bears comparison with the break-up of the marriage between Prince Charles and Princess Diana, once the supposed epitome of happiness and solidity in British public life. Their marital woes, played out on a public stage, and lapped up in newspapers and magazines around the globe, culminated in a separation and there was soon talk of another royal divorce. How could this seemingly loving couple, who had the whole nation joining in their union with a day off and street parties the length and breadth of the land, somehow break that cardinal rule of the royals – duty above self

Below: *The wedding of Prince Charles and Princess Diana was watched by millions around the world, but the fairy tale later degenerated into a story of sleaze and deceit.*

– and plunge the very existence of the monarchy into doubt?

Rumblings of unhappiness between Charles and Diana had been growing for some time. The dizzy days of 1981, when the couple married and behaved like the besotted creatures they were, had long past. The loving looks that Diana used to throw Charles with those marvellous blue eyes of hers had frozen into icy stares of contempt whenever the duo were photographed together at official functions.

A HUGE DIVIDE

Perhaps Princess Diana should have known what she was marrying into when he proposed to her. Long into their relationship she still had to address him as 'sir,' as protocol demanded, and closer scrutiny of his tastes, in everything from fashion to music to food to friends, would have shown her that there was a huge divide between them. Diana, who, as Lady Diana Spencer, first fell in love with Prince Charles when she was 16, undoubtedly put her doubts to the back of her mind, preferring to bask instead in the splendid realisation that she had bagged one of the most – if not the most – eligible bachelor in the land.

She was 20 when she married the 32-year-old Prince – an age gap that began to tell on the relationship even as the honeymoon began. The couple were aboard the Royal Yacht Brittania, cruising in the Mediterranean, away from the prying eyes of the paparazzi photographers who had made the princess the most photographed face in history.

But it was far from an intimate love-boat for two. Diana realised there and then that 'duty' came above everything and her honeymoon was spent at dinners attended by officials, while every romantic moment seemed to be interrupted by the officers of the yacht who raced around seeking to satisfy their every whim. And when Charles wasn't in the dining room or on the bridge of the vessel, he preferred to be alone, reading tracts on mysticism and the meaning of life, heavyweight tomes which had no place in either the head or the heart of the pop-loving princess.

She bore him sons and heirs, Harry and William, and played the dutiful wife at every function where she was called upon

> DIANA WAS BASKING IN THE REALISATION THAT SHE HAD BAGGED THE MOST ELIGIBLE BACHELOR IN THE LAND

Below: *Princess Diana with her sons, Princes Harry and William, on the first day of the school term.*

to do so. But the character differences soon began to tell upon them. It was noted as early as 1985 that on royal tours abroad they rarely shared the same bedroom.

Some 40 members of staff – loyal servants of Charles when he was a bachelor – were dismissed on Diana's orders in the early years. And in 1986, suffering from stress exacerbated by a slimming disease, Diana collapsed at a trade fair in Vancouver, Canada – only to suffer a stinging rebuke about her lack of dignity from her husband when she came round.

Clearly all was not well with the future King and Queen – but the public had, as yet, no inkling of just how disastrously

DIANA TOOK TO DRIVING
AROUND LONDON LATE AT
NIGHT, EITHER ON HER
OWN, OR WITH ONE OF HER
SLOANEY FRIENDS

DIANA WAS SEEN IN THE
COMPANY OF YOUNG ARMY
OFFICERS

Left: *Prince Charles with
Camilla Parker-Bowles, the
woman widely reputed to be
his mistress.*

Below: *Andrew Morton, a
tabloid reporter who turned
author and showed the royal
marriage to be a sham.*

irreparable the rift between them was growing. Diana took to driving around London
late at night, either on her own, or with one
of her Sloaney friends from her bachelor
girl days. Charles began to holiday alone –
in Italy, painting, and in the Kalahari Desert
in Botswana, Southern Africa, where he
went on a nature trek with his philosopher
friend Sir Laurens van der Post.

LARKING AROUND

The press noted that during one particular
period they spent just one day together in
six weeks. Diana was seen in the company
of dashing young army officers. One
evening in 1987 she was photographed

Above: *Diana and her sons. She has never hesitated to publicly show her motherly bond with them.*

TEARFULLY, DIANA BEGGED THE PHOTOGRAPHER FOR THE PICTURES, FEARING THEY COULD RUIN HER

'laughing and larking' as she left the home of a friend in Knightsbridge, West London, on the arm of army officer David Waterhouse. Tearfully, Diana begged the photographer for the pictures, fearing they could ruin her. The photos did not appear anywhere, but the story that surrounded their taking did – and it further cemented the rumours which were flying around.

Two years later Diana would be linked to James Gilbey, a car dealing member of the famous gin dynasty. Gilbey frequently invited Diana to his London flat – insisting, once, when she was caught out there that she was the fourth person needed to make up a bridge quartet. He was, however, completely unable to explain to reporters who had watched his residence all night, the absence of any other bridge players! Pretty soon the royal marriage was nothing more than a sham – with Diana finding solace with her own companions while Charles found his with an old friend of his called Camilla Parker-Bowles, a woman who the British public was to know well in the years to come.

Two things finally blew apart the sham marriage of the Princess of Wales and the future King. One was a book released in 1992 by journalist Andrew Morton in which the sad state of affairs was meticulously chronicled – most of it related by people whom the Princess had expressly given permission to talk.

SECRET CONVERSATION

The book chronicled suicide attempts by Diana – cries for help rather than full-blown bids at dying – her eating disorder, her dreadful row with Charles and the massive gulf which had opened up between them as a result. The second was a tape recording, made in 1989, which was buried for a couple of years before surfacing in British and foreign publications. The tape was allegedly of a conversation between Gilbey and the princess, recorded by a sophisticated listening device. More shocking than the eavesdropping was the tone of the telephone chat itself – it was clearly the talk of lovers, reminiscing of times past and arranging future trysts.

It was branded the infamous 'Squidgy' tape, Squidgy apparently being the pet name that Gilbey had given to his princess. The tape was of two conversations, recorded on New Year's Eve 1989 and on 4 January 1990, allegedly made on Gilbey's car phone to Diana at Sandringham. Here are some extracts from the phone calls that were heard around the world:

GILBEY: That's all I want to do darling. I just want to see you and be with you. That's what's going to be such bliss, being back in London.
DIANA: I know.
GILBEY: I mean, it can't be a regular feature, darling, and I understand that, but it would be nice if you are at least next door, within knocking distance.
DIANA: Yes.
GILBEY: What's that noise?

DIANA: The television drowning my conversation.

GILBEY: Can't you turn it down?

DIANA: No.

GILBEY: Why?

DIANA: Because it's covering my conversation.

GILBEY: All right... don't worry... I can tell the feeling is entirely mutual. Uuuummmmm Squidgy, what else? It's just like unwinding now. I am just letting my heartbeat come down again now. I had the most amazing dream about us last night. Not physical, nothing to do with that.

DIANA: That makes a change.

GILBEY: Darling, it's just that we were together an awful lot of time and we were having dinner with some people. It was the most extraordinary dream, very vivid, because I woke up in the morning and remembered all aspects of it. All bits of it. I remembered sort of what you were wearing and what you had said. It was so strange, very strange and very lovely too.

DIANA: I don't want to get pregnant.

GILBEY: It's not going to happen.

DIANA: (A long sigh.)

GILBEY: Don't worry about that, it's not going to happen darling. You won't get pregnant.

DIANA: I watched 'Eastenders' today and one of the main characters had a baby. They thought it was by her husband but it was by another man. Ha ha!

GILBEY: Squidgy... kiss me. Oh God, it's wonderful this feeling, isn't it? This sort of feeling. Don't you love it?

DIANA: I love it.

GILBEY: Umm.

DIANA: I love it.

GILBEY: Isn't it absolutely wonderful? I haven't had it for years. I feel 21 again.

DIANA: Well you're not, you're 33.

Later he says to her: 'Do you know, as we go into 1990, honey, I can't imagine, you know, what it was that brought us together on that night.

DIANA: No, I know.

GILBEY: And let's make full use of it.

DIANA: I know.

Diana goes on to talk about how 'tortured' her life is with Charles, about her weight, about a meeting she is arranging in London with Gilbey and small talk about going on a swimming trip soon with Fergie and their respective children. One of the conversations ends on this note:

DIANA: I'd better, I'd better. All the love in the world, I'll speak to you tomorrow.

GILBEY: All right. If you can't get me in the morning... you're impatient to go now.

DIANA: Well, I just feel guilty because I haven't done my other business.

GILBEY: Just that I have to wait until Tuesday.

DIANA: All right.

GILBEY: I'll buzz off and simply behave. I'll approach the evening with such enormous confidence now.

DIANA: Good.

GILBEY: And you darling, don't let it get you down.

DIANA: I won't, I won't.

Above: *It is all smiles for the princes and Diana on a skiing holiday in Austria, even though the royal marriage teeters on the brink of extinction.*

DIANA TALKS ABOUT HOW 'TORTURED' HER LIFE IS WITH CHARLES, ABOUT HER WEIGHT, AND ABOUT A MEETING SHE IS ARRANGING WITH GILBEY

The effect upon the marriage – coupled with the impact of the book – was electrifying. Now there could be no doubt in the minds of the British public that the end was in sight. But there would be another tragedy in the House of Windsor in this, the *annus horribilis* of Her Majesty, which was to strike before the end of 1992. On 21 November fate itself, rather than the over-sexed genes of her offspring, seemed to conspire against the Queen to cap an altogether miserable year.

That night, Windsor Castle, the most celebrated of royal retreats, guardian of the realm's treasures, was consumed by a massive blaze. It was a fire which, if there had been adequate sprinkler systems installed, might have been contained much more quickly. But the castle wasn't built as a hotel or a government office with all necessary fire exits. It was a medieval structure, scene of over 600 years of pomp and circumstance.

In the fire, sparked by a picture restorer or a loose cigarette end – the cause is still

Above: *Her Majesty the Queen – symbol of a monarchy galloping towards oblivion.*

Right: *The devastation of Windsor Castle ended 1992 – a miserable year for the Queen – she described it as her* annus horribilis.

WINDSOR CASTLE, MOST CELEBRATED OF ROYAL RETREATS, GUARDIAN OF THE REALM'S TREASURES, WAS CONSUMED BY A MASSIVE BLAZE unclear – some of the finest rooms known to British history were destroyed. Gone in the smoke and flames were many paintings, valuable woodcarvings and the magnificent St. George's Hall, scene of 600 years of state banquets. The Brunswick Tower, Chester Tower, Star Chamber and the Queen's private chapel were also severely damaged, at a cost of £60,000,000. It was a burden which the British taxpayer was expected to foot – initially.

PUBLIC ANGER

In the end, to assuage a mounting tide of anger from her subjects – many of them no doubt turned against the idea of paying for a monarchy which behaved so unregally behind the scenes – she broke with centuries of tradition and agreed to pay taxes on her considerable wealth. The restoration of the castle would not come from the public purse after all.

The fire may have destroyed the Queen's home – but it was an announcement in the House of Commons a few weeks later that burned into her heart. Following the disastrous fire, on 9 December in the House of Commons, John Major rose to deliver this statement about the collapse of the royal marriage between Charles and Diana. The House, and the nation, listened in hushed tones as he spoke: 'It is announced from Buckingham Palace that, with regret, the Prince and Princess of Wales have decided to separate.

'Their Royal Highnesses have no plans to divorce and their constitutional positions

Below: *The devastation caused by the fire was clear: one of Britain's best-loved landmarks had been irreparably damaged by the blaze.*

are unaffected. Their decision has been reached amicably, and they will both continue to participate fully in the upbringing of their children. Their Royal Highnesses will continue to carry out full and separate programmes of public engagements and will, from time to time, attend family occasions and national events together. The Queen and the Duke of Edinburgh, though saddened, understand and sympathise with the difficulties that have led to this decision.

'Her Majesty and His Royal Highness hope that the intrusion into the privacy of the Prince and Princess of Wales may now cease. They believe that a degree of privacy and understanding is essential if their Royal Highnesses are to provide a happy and secure upbringing for their children, while continuing to give a wholehearted commitment to their public duties.'

After the statement the prime minister said: 'The succession to the throne is unaf-

fected. The children of the Prince and Princess retain their position in the line of succession and there is no reason why the Princess of Wales should not be crowned queen in due course. The Prince of Wales' succession as head of the Church of England is also unaffected.'

But it was gross naïvety, or stupidity, on the part of Buckingham Palace and Downing Street to think that the speculation and debate about the future of the monarchy would subside with such a statement. In fact, the debate increased because of the notion, left hanging in the air, that Britain could have a king and queen who never speak to each other!

ROYAL HYPOCRISY

The thought of such gross hypocrisy being presented to the people of Britain set the chattering classes chattering as never before. And at the beginning of 1993 came publication of a second secret taped phone conversation which probably put paid to a King Charles and Queen Diana combination forever – the alleged chat between Charles and Camilla Parker-Bowles.

In a conversation of 1,574 words, Charles tells her that he loves her twice and she responds in a similar fashion 11 times. The conversation, recorded in 1989, two weeks before the Squidgy tape between Diana and James Gilbey, is far more lewd, and seriously damaged the credibility of the man who would be King:

CHARLES: Oh stop! I want to feel my way along you, all over you and up and down you and in and out.
CAMILLA: Oh!
CHARLES: Particularly in and out!
CAMILLA: Oh, that's just what I need at the moment.
CHARLES: Is it?
CAMILLA: I know it would revive me. I can't bear a Sunday night without you.
CHARLES: Oh, God.
CAMILLA: It's like that programme, 'Start the Week'. I can't start the week without you.
CHARLES: I fill up your tank!
CAMILLA: Yes, you do.
CHARLES: Then you can cope.
CAMILLA: Then I'm all right.
CHARLES: What about me? The trouble is I need you several times a week.
CAMILLA: Mmm, so do I. I need you all the week. All the time.
CHARLES: Oh God, I'll just live inside your trousers, or something. It would be much easier!
CAMILLA: What are you going to turn into, a pair of knickers? Oh, you're going to come back as a pair of knickers.
CHARLES: Or, God forbid, a Tampax! Just my luck!
CAMILLA: You are a complete idiot! Oh, what a wonderful idea!
CHARLES: My luck to be chucked down a lavatory and go on and on forever swirling round the top, never going down.

THE ALLEGED CONVERSATION HAD CHARLES, HEIR TO THE BRITISH THRONE, FANTASISING ABOUT BECOMING A TAMPAX

Opposite Top: *John Major announced the separation of the Waleses (below), but stipulated that Diana could still reign in Buckingham Palace (opposite bottom).*

Above: *The woman reputed to have stolen Prince Charles' heart – Camilla Parker-Bowles.*

Below: *The Queen Mother, a figure of stability amidst unrest, waves to crowds on her 86th birthday, surrounded by the rest of the family.*

I think you ought to give the brain a rest now. Night night.
CHARLES: Night darling. God bless.
CAMILLA: I do love you and I am so proud of you.
CHARLES: I am so proud of you.

There was a time when newspapers would never have dared to print anything quite so scandalous associated with the future monarch. Now is not such an age and the press broke ranks to print the whole, tawdry talk. It was the conversation which has virtually assured an end to there ever being a queen Diana sitting with Charles on the throne – that is assuming that he ever ascends to the title of King of Britain.

Just who made the tapes is still an issue, with many believing that the security services were behind them. But it is a side issue at best. What they reveal are all the petty jealousies, intrigues and scheming that have been part and parcel of the House of Windsor for years. Someone once said that for monarchy to retain its full majesty, it would be best for much of it to remain shrouded in mystery. Now there is no mystery, very little majesty and a very, very uncertain future for the most regal royal household in the world.

CAMILLA: Oh, darling!

Later in the conversation, as they begin saying an extended goodbye which seems to last forever, he says to her: 'Love you too. I don't want to say goodbye.'

CAMILLA: Well done for doing that. You're a clever old thing. An awfully good brain lurking there, isn't there? Oh darling,